Between Theory and Practice

Case Studies for Learning to Teach

Anna M. Kindler
The University of British Columbia

Salvador J. Badali
The University of British Columbia

Renée Willock
The University of British Columbia

Prentice Hall Allyn and Bacon Canada
Scarborough, Ontario

Canadian Cataloguing in Publication Data

Kindler, Anna M., 1959–
    Between theory and practice: case studies for learning to teach

Includes bibliographical references.
ISBN 0-13-082216-7

1. Teaching—Case studies. I. Badali, Salvador J., 1958– . II. Willock, Renée, 1968– . II. Title.

LB1025.3.K557 1999   371.102   C98-931300-X

ISBN 0-13-082216-7

Vice President, Editorial Director: Laura Pearson
Acquisitions Editor: Dawn Lee
Marketing Manager: Christine Cozens
Associate Editor: Sharon Loeb
Production Editor: Andrew Winton
Copy Editor: Jim Leahy
Production Coordinator: Peggy Kakaflikas
Cover Design: Dave Mckay
Cover Image: Photodisc
Page Layout: Carol Magee

13 14 15 DPC 10 09 08

Printed and bound in Canada.

Contents

Part Five: Classroom Management 73

Preface

CASE STUDY METHOD IN TEACHER EDUCATION

In recent years, case studies have increasingly been employed in a number of professional education programs. Faculties of law, medicine, and business have pioneered the problem-based approach to learning that relies heavily on the use of case studies in helping students construct their knowledge at the intersection of practice and theory. The advantage of case studies — carefully constructed accounts of actual or realistic situations — is not only in their directness, easy-to-read format, and engaging narrative that readily captures students' attention, but also in their potential to develop life-long habits of reflective practice (Carter & Anders, 1996; Wasserman, 1993).

This collection of 25 case studies, written to support the learning of beginning student-teachers, offers scenarios of classroom situations that pose questions and require answers that can be found through careful examination and application of educational theory. By providing only situations and facts that need to be analyzed and interpreted, case studies necessitate students' active involvement in learning and encourage independent study as a way to prepare for case study exploration, whether individually or in the context of "discussion teaching" (Welty, 1989).

Case study method is particularly effective in helping students make meaningful connections between theory and practice. When students are asked to solve problems and to make judgments and recommendations in regard to classroom situations presented in case studies, they become challenged to rely on more than intuitive insights and to support and justify their opinions through relevant references to educational theory. The ability to see educational theory as relevant and applicable to solving classroom dilemmas and informing teaching practice is essential for students to develop attitudes of inquiry and interest in continuing professional development.

OUR APPROACH TO CASE STUDIES: LEARNING FROM EXAMPLES, LEARNING FROM MISTAKES

We learn from both examples and mistakes. This collection of case studies includes stories about teaching that demonstrate successful practice as well as problematic classroom situations. This approach encourages students to be truly reflective and open-minded in their analysis and prevents them from assuming that their task is limited to identifying problems. In our work with student-teachers, we have found that the exclusive use of negative cases tends to develop overly critical attitudes toward practice of others and impairs students' ability to fully benefit from practicum experiences. When students are conditioned to continuously focus on problems and difficulties in teaching, they are less likely to attend to and learn from exemplary practice demonstrated by their sponsor teachers. The balanced approach adopted in this collection encourages students to begin analysis of teaching situations from an unbiased position and to draw on their knowledge of educational theory to form and justify their opinions and judgments.

FOCUS AND SCOPE OF THIS COLLECTION: BUILDING FOUNDATIONS OF PEDAGOGICAL KNOWLEDGE

Selection of instructional content is always a difficult decision and is never free of compromises. What we decide to teach is affected by a number of factors, including learners' prior knowledge, the time available to explore the selected issues, and the broader context of formal and informal education that impact on our students' learning.

The five themes selected as the focus of this collection of cases studies — the role of the teacher; instructional planning; instructional strategies; assessment, evaluation, and reporting; and classroom management — certainly do not cover all the educational concerns on which beginning teachers need to reflect. However, they tend to emerge as the key areas of concern in typical introductory teacher education courses. Learning of educational theory related to these issues helps students build prerequisite knowledge to approach more complex educational themes in insightful and meaningful ways.

For example, a basic understanding of instructional planning prepares students for discussion of planning for teaching children and adolescents for whom English is a second language and for learners with special needs, including those with exceptional abilities. Similarly, issues of gender equity or anti-racist education can be more insightfully discussed after students have acquired a fundamental understanding of teachers' social roles, responsibilities, and ethics. Recognizing that a premature introduction of cases dealing with these more complex issues would carry the risk of only superficial and intuitive analysis, we have decided not to include them in this volume, which is designed to help build only the first layer of foundations of pedagogical knowledge.

ORGANIZATION OF THE BOOK

This collection is divided into five parts, composed of thematically related case studies involving beginning teachers in Canadian primary, intermediate, middle-years, and secondary classrooms. Each case is followed by a suggested bibliography of general textbook resources related to the main theme, as well as a selection of readings pertaining directly to the focus of the case. These have been recommended to help student-teachers broaden their knowledge base, which will assist them in case analysis and help them ask and answer meaningful questions leading to the improvement of their own practice.

Although the case studies included in this volume have been written especially for beginning teachers, they also offer interesting reading to experienced teachers, especially those who work as mentors of newcomers in the field of education and wish to further reflect on the challenges facing their young colleagues at the outset of their professional careers. Case studies can be an important means of furthering reflective teaching practice, and this book seeks to make this task more accessible, more exciting, and more enjoyable.

Anna M. Kindler

REFERENCES

Carter, K., & Anders, D. (1996). Program pedagogy. In F. Murray (Ed.), *The teacher educator's handbook* (pp. 557–592). San Francisco: Jossey-Bass.

Wassermann, S. (1993). *Getting down to cases: Learning to teach with case studies.* New York: Teachers College Press.

Welty, W. (1989). Discussion method teaching. *Change*, July/August, 41–49.

Acknowledgments

We would like to extend our gratitude to the many experienced and beginning teachers whose practice and stories provided inspiration for our work. We would like to thank our colleagues and students in the Faculty of Education at The University of British Columbia, who have been involved with the Principles of Teaching course over the past two years, for their insightful comments and suggestions that helped shape this collection of case studies. We would also like to acknowledge the thoughtful advice of Dr. Charles Ungerleider, the invaluable assistance of Peggy Speidel, the much-needed secretarial help of Davinder Hothi, and all the support offered us by the UBC Faculty of Education. Finally, we wish to thank our families, and especially our spouses — Pawel Kindler, Kathleen Badali, and Brian Willock — for their encouragement and patience throughout the completion of this project. We also owe special thanks to Jan and Antoni Kindler for helping us consider children's perspectives in the creation of case studies situated in elementary classrooms.

THE ROLE OF
THE TEACHER

Part

I

ADEY'S FIRST DAYS AT CONCORDIA:
Building Student-Teacher Relationships

1

When Adey heard about her new job at Concordia Elementary, her first full-time permanent teaching position, she was overwhelmed with joy. Finally, her dream of being a "real" teacher, with her own classroom and her own group of seventh graders, was about to come true!

Not only that, but Concordia was one of the best schools in the district. Everyone wanted to teach at Concordia. Last year Adey had a chance to be a teacher-on-call there for a day, and she really enjoyed her experience. The students were not only well behaved but also attentive and curious. The teachers seemed friendly and relaxed. "This is going to be a wonderful year," she thought, as she counted the days remaining before the beginning of the school year.

Then came the bad news. Adey found out that she was hired to replace a teacher who had the reputation of being "the best." Mr. K., as the kids referred to him, was a legend. He was easy-going, friendly, ath-

letic, and humorous; he had the "magic" of teaching. For the past ten years, it had been a rite of passage for the graduating class at Concordia to move to Mr. K's. portable for the final, most spectacular year of elementary school. To make things even worse, Mr. K. had been supposed to be back in September and the returning grade 7 students fully expected him to greet them at the door. They didn't know that he had applied to a graduate school in a different province and decided to move when he received the letter of acceptance in early summer.

Not surprisingly, they were visibly disturbed and disappointed to see Adey in his place. "You're only a substitute, right?" they wanted to be reassured. "When will Mr. K. be back?" When Adey announced that she was there to stay, dead silence filled the room.

"It's a joke, right?" said a voice from the back of the room.

"They can't do this to us. To trade Mr. K. for *her*?" another student added.

This was certainly not the welcome that Adey had hoped for. Still, she was not ready to give up. She was going to meet this challenge, she tried to convince herself, scanning the room in search of a pair of sympathetic eyes. She was young, she was energetic, she played sports, and she was full of ideas. She was going to turn these kids around.

"Mr. K. is not coming back and I am really sorry about it. I know that he's been a great teacher and everyone at the school will miss him. But on the bright side of things, you could have ended up with Mrs. Gorton instead of me, so I suppose you should count your blessings!" Mrs. Gorton was one of the oldest teachers in the school, one who "should have retired years ago," as one of the teachers told her in the staff room. Mrs. Gorton did not seem to fit with the rest of the teaching team at Concordia. Her teaching methods seemed very old-fashioned. Her face was long and sad looking, and she had the reputation of being very strict. The laughter in the classroom prompted by Adey's remark made her more relaxed and confident. She would be able to find common ground with these students.

"My name is Adey," she continued, "and you can feel free to call me by my first name." She could see by her students' smiling faces that they were impressed by her invitation to call her Adey. No one in the school was allowed to address their teacher this way. "She's cool," she overheard someone remark. Adey was pleased. "I know that we are going to have a fun year together," she announced with enthusiasm.

She had just a few moments left with her students before they were to join the assembly in the gym. Adey decided to check attendance quickly. She wanted to learn students' names as soon as possible. As she started reading the names off the class list,

she noticed the background noise in the classroom increasing. "I guess I should give them an opportunity to talk before the assembly," she thought. "They have a lot to absorb today."

The next day, Adey walked to school with renewed enthusiasm. After all, her students already thought that she was a "cool teacher." As the bell rang, she was about to greet her class when she heard a student call out loudly: "Adey, can we go outside and play basketball?" a tall boy in the second row wanted to know.

"Well, I planned other activities for today," she said hesitantly.

"Come on, Adey. It's such a nice day. Let's have some fun. It's only the beginning of the year."

"Yes, Adey, let's go. Let's have some fun," another boy added.

"Okay, I guess we can do that. You are right; it's only the first full day and we can catch up later on the things I had planned for us." Adey decided to go with the flow of events. "If I want to have these kids on my side I need to be responsive to their needs," she tried to reassure herself about her decision. Before she had a chance to say anything, a small group of boys was already up and heading toward the door. "Wait a minute," she called out. She tried to slow them down, but her efforts were in vain. They were already outside of the portable and she could hear them running down the stairs.

"Do we have to play basketball?" a girl with short blond hair asked. "I hate basketball."

"What's your name?" Adey asked the girl.

"Lucille."

"Well Lucille, we just decided to go play basketball. Isn't that what everyone wanted?"

"Sure," she heard one of the students say.

"Let's go folks," said a boy in an over-sized Chicago Bulls T-shirt, trying to get the rest of his classmates outside as quickly as possible.

"You don't have to play basketball, Lucy," he reassured the girl. "No one asked you to. You're not quite a star at it, you know? You can just sit and watch or whatever." The boy in the Chicago Bulls T-shirt was now in command. "Don't worry Adey. She'll be okay."

"Ms … what is your last name?" a girl sitting next to Lucille inquired.

"Ms Aboku," Adey replied, "but you can call me Adey."

"Ms Aboku," the girl continued, apparently not comfortable with calling her teacher by her first name, "can we just stay in the classroom. I don't feel like going outside and I don't care to play basketball either."

"We should all stick together," Adey replied.

"Then why don't you have Brad and the rest of the guys come back. It's not fair that we all have to do what they want," the girl sitting next to Lucille suggested.

"I thought that you all wanted to play outside," said Adey, now on the defensive. "Not much we can do about it now. Let's go, everyone is already on the courts." Adey was getting impatient. The girls finally got up and began to walk slowly toward the door. She noted one of them roll her eyes.

As they reached the outdoor basketball court, Adey spotted Brad and his friends playing two on two. They were surrounded by a group of spectators who encouraged them in their efforts, but Adey noticed that several of her students were missing. "Where is everyone?" she wondered.

A slim girl who was chewing gum was willing to help her. "I saw Steve and Bernard walking that way," said the girl, pointing in the direction of three portables on the other side of the field. "And Erin must be in the library. She said that she wanted to talk to Mrs. Tran about something. And Marie-Lise and Wanda went to the bathroom." Adey was grateful to have such a detailed report on at least some of her missing students.

She approached the basketball court. "Okay, let's organize everyone for the game," she said, trying to get the boys' attention.

"Not now, Adey. Let's finish this game first," Brad commanded. He was about to pass his opponent on the way to the basket. Looking at him stretching to reach the hoop, Adey noticed how tall he was for his age.

The girl with the gum seemed to read Adey's mind: "Brad is older than all of us," she explained. "He transferred last year from Waterloo Heights. He has lived all over the world, and he attended international school in the Philippines. When his family moved back, they couldn't figure out what grade he should be in. They tried him in grade 7 last year but apparently he couldn't make it so they put him in grade 6. He's really cool though," she quickly added. "He's totally great at basketball, number one on the school team."

Adey was not sure what to do. She realized that she would need Brad to build a good relationship with this class. He seemed to be "the class hero," at least for some of the kids. At the same time, she was concerned that other students were just standing around watching, and it seemed that more and more of them were in fact missing from the crowd. She looked at her watch. There was still some time left before recess. "What if I join the game?" she thought. She quickly ran onto the court and grabbed a loose ball. "Here Brad, can I play too?" Her involvement clearly had a positive effect. Before she knew it, there were six other players on the court and those who were watching seemed much more involved. They cheered for her, and she felt a comfortable sense of belonging.

When the bell rang, Adey was sorry to stop the game. "We'll have to continue some other time!" she shouted, catching the ball. "See you in the classroom after the recess."

"You're pretty good at basketball." Brad turned to her as she was about to head toward the portable. Adey was very pleased with his comment.

"Are you going to coach our team this season?" another boy asked. "That would be cool."

Now it seemed that she had the whole basketball team on her side. "I wonder if even Mr. K. could have developed such a good relationship with these students so quickly," Adey complimented herself as she walked toward her empty portable to pick up her notes for the day. "Quite a few changes to be made," she sighed, glancing over her agenda for the day. "But it was well worth it. And aren't teachers supposed to be accommodating and flexible anyway?"

GENERAL REFERENCES

Arends, R. (1994). The first year of teaching: Career development and school improvement. In *Learning to teach* (pp. 451–468). New York: McGraw-Hill.

Cruikshank, D., Bainer, D., & Metcalf, K. (1995). Effective teachers: Personal attributes and characteristics. In *The act of teaching* (pp. 313–331). New York: McGraw-Hill.

Ornstein, A. (1990). The effective teacher. In *Strategies for effective teaching.* (pp. 521–572). New York: HarperCollins.

SPECIFIC REFERENCES

Gordon, R. (1997). How novice teachers can succeed with adolescents. *Educational Leadership, 54*(7), 56–58.

Hawkey, K. (1996). Image and the pressure to conform in learning to teach. *Teaching and Teacher Education, 12*(1), 99–108.

Sumara, D., & Luce-Kapler, R. (1996). (Un)becoming a teacher: Negotiating identities while learning to teach. *Canadian Journal of Education, 21*(1), 65–83.

Wesley, D. (1998). Eleven ways to be a great teacher. *Educational Leadership, 55*(5), 80–81.

TWO PORTRAITS

OF JOSELINE:

Understanding

Teaching and

Caring

AN MING LOU'S STORY

An Ming Lou is a grade 2 teacher at the inner-city Heritage Elementary School. Her students come from a variety of ethnic and socioeconomic backgrounds; several children come from single-parent families. Half of the children in An Ming's class participate in the breakfast and lunch programs designed to help meet their nutritional needs. She has been contacted earlier this year by a social worker about the difficult situations of two of her students.

While coping with the multiple needs of this diverse group of students has been a challenge for An Ming in her first year of teaching, she has embraced the challenge with enthusiasm and optimism. An Ming has always been a caring and empathic person and has experience working as a volunteer at the Women's Crisis Centre with children from dysfunctional families. She knows that she will be able to reach and extend her love to children who, in some cases, face difficult realities at home on a daily basis. She knows that she will be there for her students, helping build their self-esteem, pride, and confidence. She will give them the opportunity to share their experiences and to play and learn in a relaxed, caring, and nonjudgmental atmosphere. She will model and help them develop social skills; she will foster their enthusiasm for learning and encourage them to take risks.

One of the students in An Ming's class is Joseline. An Ming was informed that Joseline is a foster child who has been placed in the home of Patricia Hsieh after an unsuccessful adoption earlier in her life. An Ming was quick to relate Joseline's quiet and soft-spoken manner to her difficult past and made a conscious decision to focus on building Joseline's self-confidence. She was careful to praise Joseline's every effort and placed her in a cooperative learning group with Gillian and Hey Soon, with whom Joseline seemed to be good friends.

From her early interactions with Joseline, An Ming knew that this student was a bright and talented child. She was, in fact, surprised at Joseline's competency in reading, her extensive knowledge of children's books, and the beautiful drawings that filled Joseline's journal. She took the opportunity to encourage Joseline's pride in her work by openly praising her artwork and placing it on display as an example of excellent work.

As the first term neared its completion, An Ming was smiling as she filled out Joseline's report card: "Joseline is a well-adjusted, happy child," she wrote. "She is cooperative and respectful of the needs of others, and she enjoys class activities. She is a competent reader and writer, and her artwork is beautiful. I am very satisfied with her progress. It is a pleasure to have Joseline in my class." An Ming was looking forward to the parent–teacher conferences to relay the good news to Mrs. Hsieh.

PATRICIA HSIEH'S STORY

Patricia Hsieh has been Joseline's foster parent for the past three years; the little girl has become a member of her family in the fullest meaning of the word. Joseline has adjusted very well to Patricia's warm and caring home, and brings much joy into Patricia's life. She has filled the empty nest after Patricia's natural children, Sunny and Andrew, left home to study at universities on the east coast.

While soft-spoken and quiet in nature, Joseline is full of ideas that she is glad to share with others. Patricia finds her to be very social and was not surprised to see that she was quick to make friends at school. Joseline's best friends, Gillian and Hey Soon, spend at least three afternoons a week at Patricia's house.

Patricia believes that good education is the key to success in life and is closely following Joseline's progress in school. Since Joseline joined her family, Patricia has been spending a lot of time reading books to Joseline and encouraging the development of her early literacy skills. She signed her up for a number of enrichment classes, including art and music lessons, which Joseline particularly seems to enjoy.

This year, Patricia has been very disappointed with Joseline's teacher. While she likes Ms Lou as a person, she does not believe that Joseline is learning as much as she should. Joseline is certainly happy and comfortable at school, although occasionally she complains of being a little bored. However, Patricia is concerned that Joseline has not progressed at all in her reading or writing, and that her understanding of math concepts has not increased over the past four months. In art, she has served more as a teacher than a student: her drawings have been shown as examples of excellence all the time without any feedback on how to further improve her work. In the area of social studies, Joseline's knowledge remains limited to what she learned in grade one or at home, and Patricia has not seen any evidence that science is part of the grade 2 curriculum so far.

Patricia is frustrated with the lack of challenge and intellectual stimulation that grade 2 is providing her foster child. She wonders if Ms Lou is not stereotyping her daughter as an "underprivileged" child who needs to be emotionally reassured before she can learn anything. She has wanted to talk to Ms Lou for some time now, but, realizing that she is a first-year teacher, she wanted to give her some time to settle in before raising any of her concerns.

However, the recent arrival of Joseline's first-term report card makes it clear that Patricia cannot wait any longer. The report card does not contain one comment related to Joseline's academic progress, other than some check marks confirming what Patricia already knew: her daughter's ability to read and write at the level she was able to do in September. It seems obvious that the teacher's focus is not on Joseline's intellectual growth. Patricia is now determined to inquire about Ms Lou's goals and objectives and how they relate to the grade two curriculum that Patricia retrieved from the Ministry of Education's Internet site in order to be better able to support her daughter's learning. She is going to ensure that Joseline receives the kind of education she needs and deserves.

GENERAL REFERENCES

Brophy, J., & Good, T. (1986). Teacher behaviour and student achievement. In M.Wittrock (Ed.), *Handbook of Research on Teaching* (3rd ed.). New York: Macmillan.

Cruikshank, D., Bainer, D., & Metcalf, K. (1995). Three schools of thought about teaching and learning. In *The act of teaching* (pp. 51–76). New York: McGraw-Hill.

SPECIFIC REFERENCES

Brophy, J. (1983). Research on the self-fulfilling prophecy and teacher expectations. *Journal of Educational Psychology, 75*(5), 631–661.

Noddings, N. (1995). A morally defensible mission for schools in the 21st century. *Phi Delta Kappan, 76*(5), 365–368.

Solomen, D. (1996). Teacher beliefs and practices in schools serving different socioeconomic levels. *Journal of Experimental Education, 64*(4), 327–347.

3

TEAM TEACHING:
Changing Roles, Changing Responsibilities

The wind blows orange and yellow leaves against the new sign indicating that this is Brocton Middle School. The sign is the newest part of this building, which appears, at least from the outside, the same as it did when the sign read Brocton Junior Secondary School. At this time of the afternoon, when the students are all in classes, a visitor might not notice that significant changes have occurred in this school since June. Today, Brocton is a school for students in grades 6 to 8 rather than grades 8 to 10. But the fact that the students are two years younger is only the beginning of the changes that the teachers at Brocton have to contend with this year.

The school district's decision to convert Brocton into a middle school means that most teachers are teaching the same students in two or more subjects. One goal of this change is to reduce the number of different students

taught by each teacher, enabling teachers to get to know their students better. Another significant change for teachers is that most are now members of interdisciplinary teaching teams with their colleagues who teach the same students in other subject areas.

It is now the last block of the day — the prep block for one such team of teachers. This grade 7 interdisciplinary team consists of Simone, who is teaching French and English; Tracey, who is teaching science and math; and Everett, who is teaching physical education and social studies. These three teachers meet during their prep every Wednesday in the back corner of the staff room to plan and share information.

Simone: Hi. Sorry I'm late. I was talking with the librarian about giving a book talk to my advisory block.

Everett: Don't worry. I just arrived. I had to fax information about the cross-country running meet before the end of the day. It's hard losing the block of time that I used to have to get organized.

Tracey: It won't be lost time if we accomplish something in the next 45 minutes. As team leader for the week, I made an agenda for our meeting. Number one: Possibilities for integration. And two: Student concerns.

Everett: As you know, Social Studies 7 focuses on ancient civilizations. I plan to begin a unit on Egypt in November. Perhaps Simone would like to teach Egyptian myths in English to coincide with my unit.

Tracey: The pyramids suggest some interesting math problems. And the process of embalming can fit into science.

Everett: Simone?

Simone: I don't know much about mythology. My background is languages, especially French. And I was planning to really focus on establishing a writing workshop with my grade 7 English next month.

Everett: Maybe they could write myths. Or they could write about Egypt. There are many possibilities.

Simone: A key principle of the writing workshop is that students are free to write about whatever they want.

Tracey: Alright. Let's not push the integration issue. In fact, we have only been considering one form of integration. Perhaps there are other ways that we can help students make connections between their various classes. My students are already complaining that I teach math in their science block and make references to science in their math block. How did these kids develop such a rigid sense of the disciplines when they've just come from elementary school?

Everett: I'm still wondering if they should be in elementary school. I can't believe how silly some of them are. And I used to think grade eights were immature!

Simone: Speaking of immature — I am concerned about Edward Low. He's constantly disrupting the class, and the other students no longer want to work with him.

Tracey: Similar situation in my classes, especially in math. However, I have observed him focus for more than five minutes on some of the hands-on activities in science.

Everett: I get Edward to do laps around the field before social studies. It seems to settle him down. Maybe if we can get him involved in some of the lunch-hour activities in the gym, he will be better able to focus in his classes.

Simone: Good idea. Thanks Everett. It's encouraging to hear that Edward can focus under some circumstances. It's still early in the year, and he has a big adjustment to make to a new school.

Tracey: I think we are all under pressure to adjust to a "new" school. The school district has changed *who* we teach and now we need to change *how* we teach. How can we meet the needs of our students? How can we work together as a teaching team when we are all used to working independently? How can we make meaningful connections between subjects and to our students lives?

Everett: We heard about all of these issues when we attended the Middle School Conference last year. But I feel like I'm just learning by trial and error.

Simone: And I thought that after five years of teaching, I would know how to teach. I'm not sure how to deal with all of these changes this year.

Outside, the wind blows orange and yellow leaves against the new sign indicating that this is Brocton Middle School. Inside, teachers struggle with their new roles and responsibilities.

GENERAL REFERENCES

Cruikshank, D., Bainer, D., & Metcalf, K. (1995). The teacher as problem solver. In *The act of teaching* (pp. 405–421). New York: McGraw-Hill.

Ornstein, A. (1990). Professional growth. In *Strategies for effective teaching.* (pp. 573–622). New York: HarperCollins.

SPECIFIC REFERENCES

Kain, D. (1996). Recipes or dialogue? A middle school team conceptualizes "curricular integration." *Journal of Curriculum and Supervision, 11*(2), 163–187.

Lipsitz, J. (1997). Speaking with one voice: A manifesto for middle-grades reform. *Phi Delta Kappan, 78*(7), 533–540.

Martin, P. (1995). Creating lesson blocks: A multi-disciplinary team effort. *Schools in the Middle, 5*(1), 22–24.

LUNCH ROOM CONVERSATION:
Professional Ethics and Voicing Opinions

Anita Phillips, a 27-year-old student-teacher, grew up in a small community. After completing high school, she left her home town for university, where she received an honours Bachelor of Arts degree in history. After graduation, Anita was hired by the Royal Bank of Canada as a customer relations officer. She worked at a downtown branch for four years and then began a teacher education program at the university.

The first semester of teacher education had gone very well for Anita, and she had enjoyed her two-week orientation practicum placement at Riverview Secondary School. This school, with approximately 1500 students, has the support of the community. There is a general feeling among district staff and parents that good educational practice takes place at Riverview and that the school provides students with a wide range of both academic and career options.

Anita's sponsor teacher is Ms Cynthia Fleming, a teacher with twelve years' experience, all at Riverview. Over the thirteen-week extended practicum, Anita will gradually be taking over her grades 9, 10, and 11 social studies classes.

This is the first week of the extended practicum, and Anita Phillips is sitting in room 436, the location of Cynthia Fleming's grade 9 social studies class. This classroom is connected by glass partition to room 438, where Kathy Austin, a highly regarded teacher who has been at Riverview for two years, is preparing for her grade 12 civilizations class. The bell rings to signal the end of the break between the first and second periods and the beginning of class.

Jason (grade 9 pupil): Where is Ms Fleming?

Anita: I'm not exactly sure. I think she had to go down to the office to pick up copies of permission forms for the field trip to the museum in March. She should be back any minute.

Elefteria (grade 9 pupil): Are you going to teach us today Ms Phillips?

Anita: No, I'm still observing this class for a little while longer. I'm teaching Ms Fleming's other grade 9 socials class though, and I'll be taking over this class in two weeks.

Anita enjoyed talking to pupils. She found informal banter with students a wonderful way to get to know them. Before coming to Riverview, she was concerned about her ability to relate to high-school students because she was accustomed to working with adults at the Royal Bank.

Anita could see Mrs. Austin taking attendance through the glass partition while simultaneously directing students to a colourful overhead map of Western Europe. Anita didn't find room 436 very conducive to learning social studies because it was essentially a computer lab. Besides the small desk areas, the computers themselves often hid students from her view.

Anita was getting a little concerned that Ms Fleming still had not returned. Just then, a huge CRASH came from the back of the room, and Anita saw three or four students run to their seats, laughing and pointing fingers at one another. The rest of the students froze, and just as Anita was about to speak, Mrs. Austin came storming in to the classroom.

Mrs. Austin (yelling): What is going on here? You, Frank, Tina, Prabhjot, Zahara!! What have you done to that computer?

Four pupils in unison: Nothing, we were just coming in and . . .

Mrs. Austin (cutting them off in mid-sentence): Don't give me that. This isn't the first time something like this has happened. How many times have Ms Fleming and I told you that you must come into this classroom in an orderly fashion? Stop acting like

CHILDREN! Yes, CHILDREN! Start acting your age. This isn't ELEMENTARY SCHOOL! GROW UP! That's it! I want to see the four of you after this period, before lunch. Is that clear?

Four pupils (tentatively): I guess.

Mrs. Austin: What do you mean, you guess? Don't you dare leave without seeing me.

Later that day, Anita talked with two other student-teachers, Adam and Adeline, in the staff lunch room.

Anita: You wouldn't believe what happened in my period 2 social studies class this morning. This other teacher, Mrs. Austin, came storming into Ms Fleming's class and YELLS, really YELLS at four of my pupils. She went crazy because a few students had knocked over a chair. I think she thought that a computer had fallen to the floor or something.

Adam: That's nothing! Some of the students in my math class are real "weasels." They're so rude and aggressive, I can't stand them.

Anita: Okay, but this is different. They didn't really do anything and I can't understand why Mrs. Austin went off the deep end. She acted horribly. She doesn't even know these students. What gives her the right to come storming into Ms Fleming's room?

Adeline: Maybe she's taught them before and you just don't know about it. And besides, there's nothing wrong with her reprimanding another teacher's class.

Anita: I still think she acted like a bitch. When I worked at the Royal Bank as a customer relations officer, there's no way I could ever talk to a client the way she did to those students. I'd be fired on the spot! She was way out of line. And I'd heard such good things about Mrs. Austin's teaching. I guess you can't believe everything you hear. I'm just glad I don't have her as my sponsor teacher after what I saw this morning. I could never work with a person like that. That's not the kind of teacher I want to be, and I certainly don't think you gain students' respect by yelling at them. Professionals don't rant and rave. Aren't we supposed to know better?

Anita cut short what she was saying because Mrs. Lois Verplank, the vice-principal in charge of welcoming the student teachers to Riverview, was introducing Judy Anderson, the ESL department head. While Mrs. Anderson presented information about recent test scores of grade 8 and 9 students, Anita was thinking about what she had just said to her fellow student-teachers and was beginning to feel a little uneasy. Maybe she should have toned down her description of what happened. After all, there were several other teachers present in the lunch room, as well as the vice-principal. Perhaps some of them had overheard her calling Mrs. Austin a bitch. As Anita walked up the stairs to her period 3 class, she caught a glimpse of Ms Fleming and Mrs. Austin conversing quietly as they disappeared into another room.

When Anita arrived at school the next morning, she was approached by Cynthia Fleming.

Ms Fleming: Oh, good morning Anita. Do you have a minute? I'd like to talk to you about something that was brought to my attention. I'm not exactly sure how to say this.

Anita: It's about yesterday's period 2 class, isn't it?

Ms Fleming: Yes, sort of.

Anita: I'm sorry I didn't step in and handle the situation myself.

Ms Fleming: I'm not concerned with that. What really troubles me is what you apparently said about Kathy Austin.

GENERAL REFERENCES

Hargreaves, A. (1995). Realities of teaching. In L. Anderson (Ed.), *International encyclopedia of teaching and teacher education* (pp. 80–87). Tarrytown: Pergamon.

Lang, H., McBeath, A., & Hebert, J. (1995). Teaching for learning. In *Teaching: Strategies and methods for student-centered instruction* (pp. 3–24). Toronto: Harcourt Brace.

Parkay, F., Stanford, B., & Gougeon, T. (1996). Legal concerns in Canadian education. In *Becoming a teacher* (pp. 233–255). Scarborough: Allyn & Bacon Canada.

SPECIFIC REFERENCES

Bull, B. (1993). Ethics in the preservice curriculum. In K. Strike & P. Ternasky (Eds.), *Ethics for professionals in education: Perspectives for preparation and practice* (pp. 69–83). New York: Teachers College Press.

Luckowski, J. (1997). A virtue-centered approach to ethics education. *Journal of Teacher Education, 48*(4), 264–270.

Nash, R. (1991). Theme: The ethical responsibilities of teaching. *Journal of Teacher Education, 42*(3), 163–172.

Chapter 5

STUDENTS OF TEACHING:
Learning from Practicum Experiences

Max, a music student-teacher, entered room 306, where Frank, his faculty adviser, was holding the practicum debriefing meeting. Max was looking forward to talking with Frank and other student-teachers about his orientation practicum experiences. Max thought he was doing well in the teacher education program, but at the same time believed he already knew a great deal about teaching as a result of his experiences as a high-school and university student. Yet Max was just beginning to discover that teaching is more complex than he had ever imagined.

Max found a seat and looked around the room. He was impressed by the calibre of his fellow student-teachers. Sami, for example, had seven years' experience designing software for a large computer company. Lin, another student-teacher, taught English as a second language in Japan for two years before beginning the teacher education program. Denison, a business major, owned and operated a small photocopying service in Vancouver. As for Max, he had tutored four students in piano during his undergraduate years before entering the faculty of education.

After the two-week orientation practicum, Max experienced a bit of a letdown. Since returning to the faculty of education, he noticed that not all of his classmates handled the transition back to course work easily. For example, Reuben had a new baby girl to care for, Denison was looking after an elderly parent who was recently hospitalized, and Stefan worked 25 hours a week at a local restaurant. Max wondered how they were going to cope with the pressures and added workloads of the extended practicum. The extended practicum seemed like a long time away, and Max just hoped that he would survive all the assignments, tests, and exams that he had to complete this semester.

"Good afternoon," said Frank, the faculty adviser. "It's nice to see everyone together again. I would like everyone to take a few minutes to think about the rewarding as well as the challenging experiences from the practicum. I want to discuss some of the common problems that student-teachers sometimes face when they attempt to assume the role of the teacher."

After a few moments, Max was the first person to reply: "I was amazed how long it took my students to complete simple tasks. I'd plan an activity to take about 10 minutes and inevitably it would take 20 or 30 minutes. Even then, some pupils wouldn't finish. I had a hard time getting through the material." Several of the other student-teachers nodded their heads in apparent agreement.

Denison added, "My business sponsor teacher was fabulous. She had everything organized for me right from the start. She gave me seating plans, profiles of pupils, samples of their work, tons and tons of resources, and — it might seem silly —a desk in the business studies office. I've talked to some student-teachers who said they had to scramble just to find a place to work. I can't say anything but wonderful things about my sponsor teacher, I can't wait to go back!"

Max was pleased that Denison had a positive experience, but he wasn't sure if it was fair that his sponsor teacher had done all of those things for him. Before he had a chance to think about it further, Rosa, a science major, added: "I wish my sponsor teacher had been half as organized as yours. He didn't even know I was assigned to him. What I mean is that when I showed up on that first day with all the other student-teachers at the school, I was originally assigned to another person in the science department. He's nice enough but he was so busy all the time. I felt like he never had any time for

me. We hardly ever sat down and talked about what I was supposed to teach in the extended practicum. When I did teach a lesson, it's like he always gave me feedback on the run. Do you know what I mean? I was never really quite sure how well I was doing."

Max thought that Rosa was a very conscientious person and he could tell that she was a little frustrated by not knowing exactly what units she was going to teach in the extended practicum. Max wasn't sure if Rosa's situation was common or not, but his teaching loads had been negotiated and finalized before he left the practicum. If all went as planned, he was hoping to develop detailed lesson plans after Christmas for the two courses he was scheduled to begin with. Max wanted to do as much planning as possible before the start of the practicum because, as Frank warned all his student-teachers, as the practicum progressed there would be a lot less time for planning. Max was also wondering if it had been such a good idea to volunteer to help out with the music department's production of *Oklahoma!*

The next to speak was Reuben, a technology student-teacher placed in another large secondary school: "I was a little surprised to find that some of the computer software was outdated. How are kids supposed to learn how to become computer literate if they're still using old programs?"

Max remembered Reuben's glowing description of the technical institute program that Reuben had completed just before coming to the teacher education program at the university. "What I mean," Reuben continued, "is that on the one hand pupils need to know this stuff if they expect to get decent jobs, and on the other hand, school districts don't seem to have the budgets to maintain computer labs at industry standards."

"It's not just software," Denison added, "you wouldn't believe the outdated resources I saw in business studies. Some of the textbooks were published in the 1970s. I had to scour the library for decent resources, and even then I didn't have much luck. To tell you the truth, I was a little frustrated by the whole thing."

Max listened intently to both Reuben and Denison and wondered if another student-teacher was going to comment any further. Just as he was about to speak, Homa, a physical education student, spoke up: "It's not that simple. I think it's up to us to find relevant resources. I don't think we should expect school districts to provide 'teacher proof curriculum' for their teachers. If that was the case, then anybody could teach, and we know that it's not that easy."

Kara interrupted: "But how are we, as student-teachers, supposed to create lesson plan after lesson plan? I'm worried that I'm only going to be a day ahead of my pupils. I have a personal life you know. There's no way I intend to stay up all hours of the night creating lesson plans. I'll do the best I can but that's all I can do."

Max sensed that Frank was feeling a little bit uncomfortable because of some students' comments. Frank paused a moment and then asked, "Could someone share a rewarding situation from the practicum?"

Stefan, a mathematics major began hesitantly, "I want to go back to what someone said earlier about their sponsor teacher because it struck a chord with me. What happens if you can't get along with your sponsor teacher? Do you have to stay in that placement? How do you go about getting it changed?"

Frank answered Stefan's question and then tried to refocus everyone's attention. "Okay, here's what we'll do," said Frank. "I want each of you to take five minutes to write down a situation that occurred in the practicum that was a positive experience. I want you to briefly describe who was involved, as well as what you did. This will be a good way to reflect on your practicum."

GENERAL REFERENCES

Cruickshank, D., Bainer, D., & Metcalf, K. (1995). Effective teachers: Personal attributes and characteristics. In *The act of teaching* (pp. 313–332). New York: McGraw-Hill.

Knowles, J., & Cole, A. (1996). Developing practice through field experiences. In F. Murray (Ed.), *The teacher educator's handbook: Building a knowledge base for the preparation of teachers* (pp. 648–688). San Francisco: Jossey-Bass.

Lang, H., McBeath, A., & Hebert, J. (1995). Teaching for learning. In *Teaching: Strategies and methods for student-centered instruction* (pp. 3–24). Toronto: Harcourt Brace.

SPECIFIC REFERENCES

Onosoko, J. (1992). Exploring the thinking of thoughtful teachers. *Educational Leadership, 49*(7), 40–43.

Reynolds, A. (1992). What is competent beginning teaching: A review of the literature. *Review of Educational Research, 62*(1), 1–35.

Zeichner, K., & Liston, D. (1987). Teaching student-teachers to reflect. *Harvard Educational Review, 57*(1), 23–48.

Part

II

INSTRUCTIONAL PLANNING

FLUFFY RABBITS:
Deciding What
to Teach

"Did you see the display by Wendy's classroom?" Brent exclaimed, entering the staff room. "What a neat project!"

Lara, who was cleaning her coffee mug, turned around. It was a late Friday afternoon, the end of a busy week at Winterbridge Elementary. Brent and Lara, both primary teachers, were the last people left in the building, not counting George, the school engineer, whose vacuum cleaner could be heard in the background.

"You mean the fluffy rabbits?" she asked with a puzzled look on her face. Even though she taught in a different wing of the school, Lara had already noticed the latest art by Wendy's class. The display board was covered with green sheets of 10 × 12" construction paper, each featuring a white rabbit-like shape made of cotton balls. Half of the rabbits had an additional triangular orange piece of construction paper added to the composition, which Lara interpreted as a carrot. The sign in the middle of the board announced: "Happy Spring."

"Yes, aren't they fun?" Brent replied. "I'll have to ask Wendy if she has any cotton balls left. I still have plenty of white glue left over from the blocks project that Amy did with my class in December. You know, I was trying to figure out what to do for a Spring/Easter theme and these rabbits will be perfect." Brent could hardly contain his enthusiasm. "This will take care of my art lesson for next week!" Suddenly troubled by Lara's silence, Brent inquired, "Hey, Lara, is something wrong?"

"No, I'm fine," Lara replied, a big smile confirming the sincerity of her answer. "Would you like a cup of coffee before I clean up the carafe?"

"Thanks, that would be great," Brent replied. "I can't wait for the weekend to begin. It's just a miracle that Wendy posted this project. Just yesterday Chandra called me to her office and told me that a couple of parents from my class came to see her and complained that I am not good at teaching art. Can you believe that?" Brent's tone of voice conveyed his outrage. "If parents come to the principal to complain about art, what will come next? Anyway, at least for now my problem is solved. I just need to get these cotton balls from Wendy and then everyone watch out! The class of Brent Chester Hilston will be up to Wendy's rabbit challenge!" Brent leaned back on his chair, almost spilling some of his coffee.

Lara knew better than to interrupt Brent's monologue. She noticed a long time ago that when Brent's mind was engaged in a story, he had a hard time paying attention to what others had to say. She also did not want to spoil his good mood by voicing her reservations about Wendy's project. After all, the weekend was about to begin, and he had a right to fully enjoy it.

Brent, in his first year of teaching, has been a great colleague. His energy, enthusiasm, and great humour have been greatly appreciated by Lara, who has taught at the Winterbridge Elementary for fifteen years now. She wanted to support Brent in his teaching efforts, yet as an experienced teacher she also felt some responsibility to help Brent improve his practice.

Lara's continued silence prompted Brent back to the topic of Wendy's students' display. "So, Lara, what do you think? Will this take care of my art curriculum problem?" This question gave Lara the opportunity she had been waiting for: "To tell you the truth, I don't think it will, Brent," she replied.

"What do you mean?" Brent asked with slight anxiety in his voice. "Look, it is a great project, easy to do, and every child can be successful. It relates well to the theme of Spring and Easter. It looks like I have all the materials that I will need: construction paper, glue, and, well, even if Wendy does not have any leftovers, I can pick up a few bags of cotton balls on my way to school. It will only cost me a few bucks."

"You're missing the point, Brent," Lara began, only to be interrupted before she could finish her sentence.

"Okay, you don't like the project! Come on, Lara, just because you haven't done this activity with your class doesn't make it a bad art idea. It is all a matter of personal aesthetic preference." Brent was clearly on the defensive.

"This has nothing to do with aesthetic preferences, Brent. This has to do with teaching, with curriculum," Lara calmly replied.

"What do you mean?" Brent's question was accompanied by the loud ring of the staff room phone.

Lara quickly picked up the receiver. "Oh, hi. Yes, I know, it's getting late. Turn the stove on; I'm on my way." Turning back to Brent, Lara explained, "I have to rush. My family wants to reclaim me for the weekend. She hastily gathered her belongings and grabbed her jacket from the coat rack. "Sorry Brent, if you'd like we can talk about the fluffy rabbits next week. Have a good weekend."

As the door behind Lara closed, Brent got up and picked up his briefcase. He wished Lara had explained why she didn't share his enthusiasm for Wendy's project. Her comment about "teaching and curriculum" sounded so serious. "It's not going to be a worry-free weekend, after all," Brent thought with regret, as he shut the door to the staff room. On his way out, he briefly stopped in front of Wendy's art display. "What could be wrong with these fluffy bunnies?" he wondered. "They make such a great display!"

GENERAL REFERENCES

Cruickshank, D., Bainer, D., & Metcalf, K. (1995). Planning instruction. In *The act of teaching* (pp. 127–162). New York: McGraw-Hill.

Lang, H., McBeath, A., & Hebert, J. (1995). Planning for teaching. In *Teaching: Strategies and methods for student-centered instruction* (pp. 51–78). Toronto: Harcourt Brace.

Ornstein, A. (1990). Instructional planning. In *Strategies for effective teaching* (pp. 463–520). New York: HarperCollins.

SPECIFIC REFERENCES

Eisner, E. (1990). Creative curriculum development and practice. *Journal of Curriculum and Supervision, 6*(1), 62–73.

Frieberg, H., & Driscoll, A. (1996). Planning for instruction: Visualizing what could be. In *Universal teaching strategies* (pp. 21–55). Toronto: Allyn and Bacon.

Reiser, R., & Walter, D. (1996). Planning instructional activities. In *Instructional planning: A guide for teachers* (pp. 45–66). Boston: Allyn and Bacon.

C h a p t e r

7

FLYING SAUCERS:
Organizing for
Instruction

"What an exhausting day! Exhausting, but exciting," said Andrea to her roommate Terry. The two women, both in their late twenties, have been sharing a small apartment since they first met in the teacher education program at university three years ago. Andrea, who always wanted to be a teacher, was at first taken aback by what she interpreted as Terry's lack of enthusiasm for teaching. While Andrea was full of energy, with ideas flowing through her head faster than she could describe them in words, Terry was calm and composed, and rarely volunteered any ideas. Andrea's communication style was lively and dynamic; Terry spoke slowly and thoughtfully. When Andrea heard her give a short speech at the beginning of their communications course, she wondered how Terry's soft voice would ever manage to dominate in a busy classroom.

Some of their classmates were very surprised when Andrea and Terry ended up as roommates. But Andrea and Terry found out that their different personalities were more compatible than they had initially expected, and they were glad to have each other's support now that they had started their teaching careers. Both worked with intermediate grades in two different elementary schools. Terry had a fourth-grade class, while Andrea's class was a four/five split.

Terry had a way of getting on Andrea's nerves when she failed to share Andrea's excitement about her teaching experiences. As much as Andrea appreciated Terry's help preparing charts and other visual displays and her willingness to share her detailed lesson plans, she wished that Terry would appreciate her own dynamic style and her great ability to improvise. While Terry had never made any direct critical comments, Andrea felt that her roommate's reserved responses to her teaching stories were not simply a reflection of Terry's calm personality, but that they carried a negative message.

"So, what happened today?" Terry asked.

"Oh, it's a long story!" Andrea replied. "Are you ready for it?" Terry smiled. Could she not be ready? Before Terry could reply, Andrea had already began her story. "Remember, Terry, my students have just completed their space glossaries for the science unit. Goodness, I forgot to bring them home again," she suddenly exclaimed, searching without success in her large gym bag that contained several pounds of books, notes, and student assignments. "I need to clean out this bag one of these days. I don't know what I have in here anymore," she confessed.

"Anyway," said Andrea, returning to her story, "they are absolutely magnificent. Not only do they prove that the kids understood the concepts, but they are totally creative. The drawings they made are absolutely wonderful. My idea for them to make the pop-up universe pages worked out so well. The kids loved working on this project, and if you ask them about the solar system they are the experts in the school."

Terry knew that Andrea was not exaggerating. She envied her roommate for her ability to get students excited about learning to the point that they seemed to be absorbing knowledge like sponges. When Andrea's projects worked, they worked beautifully. The trouble, in Terry's opinion, was that at least half of Andrea's great ideas have failed miserably to result in desirable learning outcomes. She tried to alert Andrea to what seemed to be the major obstacle to more consistent success, but Andrea remained oblivious to her gentle hints. "Well, maybe some things just can't be changed," Terry thought, reminding herself of her own unsuccessful efforts to emulate Andrea's zestful approach to teaching.

"One of the students chose to include in her glossary a story about the UFOs and, to make a long story short, I decided that we would make papier-mâché flying saucers for this week's art lesson. We haven't experimented with this technique, and since it is one of the materials recommended for intermediate grades, I figured this would work out just fine. Also, we haven't worked on any 3-D projects this year, and I remembered that it was one of the areas suggested in the art curriculum document.

"Just the other day, Thelma mentioned that she had lots of papier-mâché paste left over from a project her grade 5 students did last week, so the timing seemed just perfect. Yesterday I asked Thelma if she still had any paste left and she told me that I could have whatever was left in two large buckets that she had put in the storage room. I was too busy to check how much was left yesterday, but from what Thelma told me I figured we should have enough. We have been collecting newspapers all term, so I knew we would have enough material for this project. For homework, I asked my students to make sketches of their saucers. This morning they were all ready to go. I told them to spread newspapers on their desks and went to get the paste buckets.

"When I opened the lids of the buckets, I almost dropped dead from the smell! Terry, it was the most atrocious odour you can imagine. I looked down and there it was: a thick layer of some mouldy stuff, more or less in the colours of the rainbow. This stuff was unusable. Everything, including the buckets, had to be thrown away. As I opened the windows, I tried to figure out what to do instead. I had planned to work on this project for most of the day, and I really did not have a backup plan ready.

"I decided to capitalize on the excitement that the mouldy growth had generated, so I sent the kids to the library to do a little research on moulds. Imagine the pressure I was under trying to come up with a more-or-less coherent assignment on the spot. I divided the class into three teams. One group was supposed to find the answer to the question 'What is a mould?' the second 'What promotes mould growth?' and the third was to find some information about 'good moulds and bad moulds.'

"I crossed my fingers as I took my class to the library, hoping that no other teacher had a class already working in there. I was lucky! Harinder, our librarian, was all alone. Needless to say, she was not very pleased to see us come with no advanced warning; but when I explained to her my emergency situation, she agreed to help. She is really a wonderful woman. She has helped me already at least three times this term when I had to operate in 'damage control' mode.

"As the students were busy surfing the Web and going through the books in the library, I decided to look for ways to still do the art project, as planned , after recess. If only I remembered what was needed to make the papier-mâché paste! Luckily, Fred had his prep time this morning and was sitting in the staff room going over his plans for a science experiment. Fred majored in art for his BA, so he was just the right person to ask. It turned out the only thing I really needed to get was flour.

"I went straight to Cheryl's classroom. Cheryl loves baking with her students, so I knew I could count on her to have some flour handy. When I entered Cheryl's classroom, she was busy explaining pie graphs to her students. But she didn't seem to be bothered too much by my interrupting her talk as she pointed to the cupboard at the back of the classroom. Her students were curious about why I needed the flour. 'Are you going to make muffins?' Ping asked. When I started to explain my project, Cheryl cut in by saying, 'All right, kids, enough of papier-mâché saucers. Let's get back to our pie graphs.' I took her hint and quickly left

her classroom carrying two large bags of flour. I found an empty bucket in the janitor's closet and, following Fred's instructions, I quickly mixed the paste. This time it looked perfect; no moulds in sight!

"I rushed to the library to see how my kids were doing. The first group seemed to be finished, while the others were still busy working on their projects. When the recess bell rang, two of the groups still had a way to go to complete their reports. Too bad I couldn't let them go back to the library after recess. We needed to start on the art project right away, otherwise we wouldn't finish it today. I told my students that they would need to complete their research on moulds as a homework assignment. Troy complained, of course, that some of the students ended up with no homework while others had so much to do. You know Troy, he's always the first one to complain.

"Anyway, as I looked at the students' sketches of flying saucers, it became obvious that most of them wanted to make rather large, platelike forms. It dawned on me that we would need some sort of support for their sculptures. Plates would be perfect, I thought. I told the class to start ripping newspapers into strips and called on Jan and Nathan to come with me to borrow some plates from the staff room. Luckily, we found enough plates so that each student could have one.

"From then on, everything went smoothly. I demonstrated the papier-mâché technique, showing them how to criss-cross the stripes on the plates to make their sculptures sturdy. We brainstormed ways to build scaffoldings to help make their saucers more three dimensional. In the end, it looks like it will be a very successful project!

"But as you can imagine, after all this excitement, I am quite exhausted," said Andrea as she sunk into the couch.

Terry had listened attentively to Andrea's story. She was used to these long monologues that captured both Andrea's best and most questionable qualities as a teacher. She wondered for a moment if she should take this opportunity to bring the latter to Andrea's attention, but looking at her roommate's tired face, she simply acknowledged that after a day like that Andrea needed some rest.

GENERAL REFERENCES

Arends, R. (1994). Planning. In *Learning to teach* (pp. 39–71). New York: McGraw-Hill.

Kindsvatter, R., Welen, W., & Ishler, M. (1996). Planning for teaching. In *Dynamics of effective teaching* (pp. 142–177). White Plains: Longman.

Ornstein, A. (1990). Instructional objectives. In *Strategies for effective teaching* (pp. 211–261). New York: HarperCollins.

SPECIFIC REFERENCES

Perrone, V. (1994). How to engage students in learning. *Educational Leadership, 51*(5), 11–13.

Posner, G., & Rudnitsky, A. (1986). *Course design: A guide to curriculum development for teachers*. New York: Longman.

Wragg, E. (1995). Lesson structure. In L. Anderson (Ed.), *International encyclopedia of teaching and teacher education* (pp. 207–211). Tarrytown: Pergamon.

THE BLACK EYE:
Capturing "Teachable Moments"

"Goodness, Lee, what happened to your eye?" Amy greeted Lee as they sat down for lunch in the school cafeteria.

Both Amy and Lee were student teachers halfway through their extended practicum at the Queensland Elementary School, a small school with a reputation for academic excellence. Amy was placed in a fourth grade classroom and had developed an excellent working relationship with Salina, an experienced teacher who was full of energy and enthusiasm and always open to new ideas. Lee was working with a sixth grade class and was having difficulties with his sponsor teacher.

Lee envied Amy for the support and encouragement she received from her mentor. His sponsor teacher, Bev, seemed very rigid and inflexible. To Lee she was painfully well organized and systematic, and he found her calm composure very intimidating. It

seemed that every time Lee proposed a change to a lesson plan that Bev had suggested, she found ways to persuade him to abandon his idea. While Amy was encouraged to plan and implement her own lessons, Lee felt constrained by having to follow Bev's lead. Even though it was true that the few lessons he initially tried had not been very successful, Lee felt that he should be given more freedom to experiment. He was tired of Bev saying that he needed to be more thorough in his planning and more conscientious about his objectives and rationale for his teaching. He feared that Bev's claims that she can appreciate spontaneity as long as it does not compromise the quality of education that her students receive were just empty words.

To be fair, Lee had to recognize that Bev did not have a reputation for being a boring teacher. When he managed to put aside his resentment, he couldn't help notice that Bev's lessons were more dynamic, creative, and fun than he would have expected from a person who seemed to lack imagination.

"Your eye, Lee, what happened to it?" Amy repeated her question as they were putting down their lunch trays. Lee's left eye was surrounded by dark black, purple, and green circles.

"Last night I went to play squash with Jeremy; the rest you can imagine," said Lee as he moved his arm through the air following the trajectory of the squash ball that had hit his face.

"Why didn't you wear protective goggles? You're impossible, Lee. You always get into trouble!" said Amy, rolling her eyes.

"Speaking of trouble, this eye thing is nothing compared to what I did today." Lee was glad to have the opportunity to talk to Amy about the chance that he took this morning by changing his approved lesson plan at the last minute and, most of all, about his fear of Bev's reaction to his unusual decision.

Amy gave Lee a curious look. "It's only lunch time and you've already gotten in trouble today?" She was smiling, trying to reduce Lee's obvious anxiety.

"I'm not kidding, Amy. I think I really messed up this time. Bev won't let me get away with it. And when I think that my mid-practicum evaluation conference is happening next week, I can't believe that I actually followed through with this idea of mine. I'm a fool, Amy, a real fool!" The tone of Lee's voice made it clear to Amy that he was indeed seriously concerned about what had happened in his classroom in the morning.

"Do you want to tell me about it?" She didn't need to repeat her question twice. Lee was more than ready to relieve his anxiety, and Amy had always been a very supportive friend.

"You see, my students are now working on a novel study unit. They read a new

chapter every two days and then do different activities designed to enhance their comprehension and response skills and to improve their ability to communicate their ideas. This week we have been working on adjusting the degree of formality in their language to suit the form and purpose of their writing. I have already had them find examples of such variation within the novel, and today they were supposed to write their predictions for the next chapter in the form of a letter to a friend. I had everything carefully planned; I even wrote samples of prediction letters and made them into overheads. Never mind the list of objectives, of course! To tell you the truth, last night when I was packing all this stuff into my backpack I felt like I was turning into another Bev! What a scary thought!"

"Come on, Lee. Give Bev a break. I know that she's not one of your favourite people, but you have to admit that she is an excellent teacher. It's enough to see her students' work. They do so remarkably well. And it's not that they suffer in the process. Did you see the pile of cards and presents she got from her kids for Christmas? They really love her, Lee. Anyway, so what happened this morning?"

"Well, I arrived at school half an hour before the kids to get myself ready for the day. When I went to straighten Celine's desk I noticed a piece of paper on the floor that somehow escaped the janitor's attention last night. I picked it up and, without much thought, read the note that one of my students must have written yesterday. It said something about this class getting to be boring because we have been working on the same novel for three weeks now. It ended with the words *I hope he'll give us a break. If I have to write one more chapter prediction I am going to throw up!* As I was reading the note it dawned on me that this student was probably expressing the sentiments of many of the students in my class.

I've been getting a feeling lately that their energy and enthusiasm for the novel is waning, that their writing is becoming less creative, as though they were just sick and tired of the topic. This kid was right — they needed a break!

"As I was scrambling for the idea to solve this problem, Bev rushed into the room. For once I was glad to see her — I really needed her advice. But as soon as I looked at her, I knew that it would not be a good idea to ask any questions at this time. Bev looked upset, and the very fact that she arrived later than usual was a clue to me that something was wrong. As if reading my thoughts, Bev explained that she had witnessed a serious car accident and that she needed to phone the police right away to make a report. 'I'm sorry, Lee, we won't have a chance to go through our morning routine,' she said as she rushed out of the class. 'But I will be back by the time the bell rings,' she assured me.

"Just about then, Tania, who always comes in first, walked into the classroom, and instead of the usual greeting looked at me with her eyes wide. 'What happened to your eye, Mr. Chow?' she exclaimed. Amy, this was when I changed my plans for the day. Forget the novel, I decided. I will have them write a story about my eye. I will divide the class into three groups: reporters, friends, and poets. Reporters will be asked to invent a story about my black eye and write it as a news item. Students in the second group will write a letter to a friend telling about my predicament, and the poets will have to describe what happened to me using poetic devices. I told Tania that she will have to wait for the explanation.

"I quickly searched for my notes from last week to be ready to give a brief review session on the use of poetic devices. I was glad to find the chart that I made for the poetry lesson three weeks ago. I guess Bev's organization has some benefits — she insisted that I put the chart in a drawer labelled 'teaching aids.' Thank goodness, I had it now. As the kids were gathering in the classroom, each of them asking me about my eye, I was becoming more and more confident that my plan would work. I glanced through my objectives overhead and was further assured that I was on the right track. The expected learning outcomes could still be achieved under my new scenario.

"Just before the bell rang, Bev returned to the classroom. She seemed more relaxed now and gave me a faint smile as I raised my hand to get the students' attention. Before I had a chance to begin the lesson, Robin, who entered the classroom as the bell rang, shouted from the back row: 'Hey, Mr. Chow, what happened to your eye?' I tried not to look at Bev as I gave myself the final go-ahead for the new lesson plan.

"Amy, you wouldn't believe the students' enthusiasm and excitement about this new project. Because I anticipated that they might be eager to exchange their views, I started by giving the students five minutes to discuss in pairs their ideas about my black eye. When their excitement had somewhat diminished, I brought them together and explained the day's assignment. I quickly presented the lesson's objectives to make it clear what they should be focusing on while working on their stories and reviewed the relevant material.

"I told them that the evaluation scheme will be the same as the one that was used when they were practising writing news articles, letters, and poems earlier this term. I showed the overheads of the appropriate evaluation forms, including the peer-evaluation sheet that they were now familiar with completing. I was glad no one complained about their group assignment. They laughed when I asked all kids with dyed hair to be poets: as you know there are quite a few of those in my class! All the journalists had to wear glasses. Everyone laughed when

Clara put on her sunglasses to join this group."

"Did you let her make the switch?" Amy asked.

"Sure," Lee replied. "I saw no reason not to. Anyway, everyone got right to work. I could hear occasional laughs and giggles as they were writing their stories. They were all so engaged in their work, I felt that their enthusiasm for writing was back! I still have to read their stories, but just by glancing at them I have a feeling that they have done really well. Before the bell rang, I explained that they will be reading each other's stories tomorrow. I left them in suspense about my eye. I told them that whoever's story is the closest to what actually happened will win a special prize. I have to remember to bring a chocolate bar tomorrow."

Amy was pleased to hear the enthusiasm and excitement in Lee's voice. "So, then, what's the problem?" she asked when Lee seemed to have reached the end of his story.

"You must be kidding!" Lee replied. "Can't you see? Bev will kill me for changing my lesson plan. She is so, so ... I don't know how to put it, but there isn't an ounce of spontaneity in her bones. Also, she will be upset that I didn't tell her about my plans ahead of time. I'm sure she's the type of person who hates surprises."

"You're really funny with your ideas about Bev," Amy interrupted. "It seems that your imagination works at least as hard on this front as it did for your students this morning. What did she say to you after the class?"

"Nothing, that's just it. Nothing! When I looked at her she had this enigmatic smile on her face and then she just said that she had to go to the police station during lunch. I was still surrounded by the kids who wanted to tell me their stories, so I really couldn't find out her reaction. I have a bad feeling though. Perhaps I should have stuck to my original plan and continued with the novel."

Before Amy had a chance to reply, Mae-Ying and Kate came to their table. "This morning was great Mr. Chow," Kate said.

"I hope you'll like my poem," Mae-Ying added, curling a string of her purple hair.

"Hey, Mr. Chow, what happened to your eye?" yelled Travis, a tall seventh grader who was on Lee's basketball team.

"It depends who you ask," Amy replied, her words drowned out by the laughter of Mae-Ying, Kate, and Lee.

GENERAL REFERENCES

Arends, R. (1994). Planning. In *Learning to teach* (pp. 39–71). New York: McGraw-Hill.

Ornstein, A. (1990). Instructional objectives. In *Strategies for effective teaching* (pp. 211–261). New York: HarperCollins.

Yinger, R., & Hendricks-Lee, M. (1995). Teacher planning. In L. Anderson (Ed.), *International encyclopedia of teaching and teacher education* (pp. 188–192). Tarrytown: Pergamon.

SPECIFIC REFERENCES

Delamont, S. (1995). Teachers as artists. In L. Anderson (Ed.), *International encyclopedia of teaching and teacher education* (pp. 6–8). Tarrytown: Pergamon.

Russell, T., & Munby, H. (Eds.). (1992). *Teachers and teaching: From classroom to reflection.* New York: The Falmer Press.

Strong, R., Silver, H., Robinson, A. (1995). What do students want and what really motivates them? *Educational Leadership, 53*(1), 8–12.

PRESSURE COOKER:

From Lesson Planning to Classroom Reality

It's 8:40 a.m. and Krista Bowman is tired. Now eight weeks into her thirteen-week practicum, Krista has been teaching three blocks of Applied Skills 8 and one block of Clothing and Textiles 9–11, in addition to the two blocks of Foods and Nutrition 9/10 that she has taught since the end of January. She appreciates the fact that her teaching assignment has increased gradually because she has used the time to plan her units. Still, at an 80 percent teaching load, Krista is feeling a little overwhelmed by the amount of preparation required for each lesson.

This morning she arrived at school early to receive a delivery of groceries because she needed fresh produce for the stir-fry lab, which was part of her vegetable unit for Foods and Nutrition 9/10. On the last class before spring break, Krista had demonstrated the recipe and then allowed each of the six groups of four students to select a different combination of vegetables to use in the stir-fry. Her A block had completed the lab before spring break and her C block would do the lab first thing this morning. She finished portioning the sauces and noodles and set out the selection of vegetables on the supply table. Although she felt rushed, Krista was pleased that she had the supplies ready by the time the bell rang.

"Good morning. I hope you all had a good spring break," Krista addressed her Block C students. She noted that students always take longer to get organized first thing Monday mornings. As she waited for their attention, Krista reminded herself to project her voice to the back of this long, narrow foods lab and to be careful that eye contact with the students was not blocked by counters and appliances. Such are the challenges of home economics teachers, thought Krista. Eventually, she focused the students on the task at hand: preparing, cooking, and eating a stir-fry as well as completing self-evaluation sheets and cleaning up in the 45 minutes that remained of the 55-minute block.

Krista knew that time was always a pressure during labs, but this class was worse than usual. The students seemed confused about the procedures and kept calling for her assistance. As Krista rushed from group to group to solve the students' problems, she became increasingly frustrated. "Remember, I demonstrated how to julienne last class!" The students were grumpy, too, especially when they realized that they would not have time to eat before cleaning up. The bell rang as Krista hurried from kitchen to kitchen, checking the quality of the stir-fry and the cleanup.

Krista spent the rest of the morning with her Applied Skills 8 classes in the sewing room on the other side of the school, but lunch hour found her back in the foods lab. She was sorting through some of her sponsor teacher's resources about vegetarianism when Tien, a student-teacher in technology education, poked his head in the door. "I was hoping to microwave this pasta," he said, smiling. "Leftovers from last night."

"Sure, help yourself," replied Krista without looking up.

Tien placed his lunch in the microwave and turned back to Krista. "So this is where you hang out at lunch. You're never in the staff room."

"Who has the time! Lately I need every waking moment just to stay on top of things. In fact, I'm beginning to feel like it's a losing battle."

"What's wrong?" Tien asked

"I don't know," Krista replied. "Take, for example, my first block this morning. I put in so much preparation time and then my stir-fry lab was a disaster. The students were so disorganized and negative. I felt like screaming at them. I think I need more sleep."

"I thought they loved to cook," Tien said.

"I thought so, too," Krista responded. "Foods is an elective; they chose to take the course. Actually, you're right. These students do like cooking, and they are usually much more cooperative and efficient than they were today. Maybe it's me. I know I'm feeling a bit stressed."

"All the student-teachers are feeling the pressure of teaching six blocks," Tien assured her.

"Well, I'm trying to be organized. I laid out all my demonstrations and labs for each unit before I got so busy. It's unfortunate that the stir-fry demonstration happened a week before the lab for Block C, but that's just the way my unit plan worked out with the school schedule."

"Couldn't you have done something else with C block before spring break so that you could do the demonstration closer to the lab?" asked Tien.

"Then Block C would be two classes behind Block A," replied Krista. "And besides, what else could I have done? The students hate worksheets, and since our curriculum and instruction courses at university emphasized active learning so much, I'm reluctant to create fill-in-the-blank exercises or word searches. So, besides a demonstration or a lab, what else could I do?"

GENERAL REFERENCES

Arends, R. (1994). Planning. In *Learning to teach* (pp. 39–71). New York: McGraw-Hill.

Cruickshank, D., Bainer, D., & Metcalf, K. (1995). Planning instruction. In *The act of teaching* (pp. 127–162). New York: McGraw-Hill.

Kindsvatter, R., Welen, W., & Ishler, M. (1996). Planning for teaching. In *Dynamics of effective teaching* (pp. 142–177). White Plains: Longman.

SPECIFIC REFERENCES

Anderson, L., & Torrey, P. (1995). Instructional pacing. In L. Anderson (Ed.), *International encyclopedia of teaching and teacher education* (pp. 212–214). Tarrytown: Pergamon.

Kagan, D. (1992). Professional growth among preservice and beginning teachers. *Review of Educational Research, 62*(2), 129–169.

Yinger, R. (1980). A study of teacher planning. *Elementary School Journal, 80*(2), 107–127.

PHOTOGRAPHS OF WAR:
Exploring a Planning Process

David Pang, a social studies student-teacher, was nearing the end of a very successful extended practicum at Jackson Heights Secondary School. Overall, the last eleven weeks had been immensely satisfying for David because he really enjoyed working with adolescents and with other teachers. As David drove home on the next-to-last Friday of the practicum, he was a little apprehensive about returning to the faculty of education to complete his course work.

Although David and his sponsor teachers were satisfied with his performance during the practicum, he wanted to plan something a little different for next Thursday's History 12 class. They were finishing off a two-week unit on the Vietnam war. Recently, he watched a television documentary about Vietnamese refugees because he thought he might pick up some good ideas for his class. After watching the

program, he thought he might do a lesson using photographs of the Vietnam war.

During the practicum, David had done a good job adapting the curriculum for his students. Initially, he was surprised to discover that even with grade twelves, there was quite a bit of difference between those he considered his best students and those who struggled with the content and course requirements. The one thing that David appreciated from his students, however, was their willingness to participate in his classes and to ask questions. David liked the students' diligence and he always looked forward to teaching them.

On Saturday, David went to the public library and browsed through books in the history section. Although it was an impractical way to plan, he enjoyed browsing in libraries because it usually inspired him to develop creative lessons for his students.

Before David knew it, two hours had passed since his arrival at the library and he was still no further ahead in his planning, other than having selected eight books about Vietnam. He was beginning to feel that maybe this wasn't such a good idea and that perhaps he should just get on with his planning and go home.

The next afternoon, David looked through some of the books he had signed out of the library and his eye was drawn to a collection of photographs contained in a Time-Life publication. Initially, all that David had decided was that he wanted his students to look at some photographs, but he wasn't sure about anything else.

"Think," David muttered aloud. Just then, Angela, his wife, entered the room. Angela was a great source of inspiration and David respected her opinions. She has been teaching grades 6/7 for two years at a local elementary school in the neighbourhood where they live.

"Do you have any ideas about how I can plan this lesson?" David asked.

"What are you thinking of doing?" asked Angela.

"Well, I have these great photographs. Look at this, here's that famous one of the South Vietnamese soldier holding a pistol to the head of a civilian in Saigon. Here's another one of an American soldier's personal possessions and wallet scattered in the mud of some battlefield. This photograph received a lot of media attention, but it was later revealed that the photographer had arranged all of the items. He didn't just stumble across the wallet, although that's how it was presented to the American public."

"Maybe," Angela suggested, "you could ask them a series of questions about each photograph."

"What if I put students in groups and asked them to analyze a photograph of their choice?" David added.

"Maybe, but do you have enough material to distribute? And besides, they might not pick a very good photograph. I think it's important that you exercise some control over what photograph they look at."

"I guess I need to think this through more clearly," said David.

Twenty minutes later, Angela rejoined David at the kitchen table.

David: Here's what I think I'm going to do. I've selected these four photographs. I'm going to make one overhead transparency for each of the photographs. I'll ask my students to focus on the image and identify what they think is happening, as well as make predictions about what they think will happen next. For example, in the photograph of the South Vietnamese soldier with the pistol, I'll ask them who they think these people are. I'm willing to bet that everyone in the class will mistakenly assume that the soldier is from communist North Vietnam. I'll ask my students to make predictions, and after some discussion I'll tell them what actually happened. I remember most of this stuff from my undergraduate courses.

Angela: Sounds good so far but I'm not entirely clear about the purpose of this lesson.

David: I want my students to critically examine what appears to be objective evidence of an event and to think about whether or not these photographs are examples of objective reporting by the mass media.

Angela: Okay, but how are you going to get their attention at the beginning of the lesson?

David: I've been thinking about this a lot. They're a really good class. I thought I would dress up in jeans, tie-dyed T-shirt, love beads, an earring, and anything else from the 60s. When they come into the classroom, I'll greet them and I will also have the John Lennon song "Give Peace a Chance" playing on the tape recorder.

Angela: Sounds great!

David: In the first ten minutes of the lesson, I want the students to guess what type of character I'm trying to portray. I'll try to elicit from them some of the things they already know about the 1960s and the Vietnam war. I'd like them to consider pop culture stereotypes, movies, books they've read, and so on. Remember, we've been studying the Vietnam war for the last three classes. This isn't entirely new material. I also want them to think about how people's attitudes toward major events like the Vietnam war are influenced by the mass media. I think I'll have a lot of fun doing this lesson.

Angela: This sounds good to me. Then what?

David: Then I'll show the entire class the photographs on the overhead, one at a time. I'll take them through each photograph and ask them a series of questions like: Who do you think the people are in the photograph? What do they appear to be doing? When do you think the photograph was taken? What do you think the reaction might have been to this photograph in the United States? in Canada? What social and economic events were occurring in the United States at the same time?

Angela: I'm still wondering about whether or not your students have enough background information to make sense of these photographs.

David: I think they do. I've thought a lot about that when planning this lesson because if they don't have the background knowledge, I don't think this lesson will work very well.

Angela: How long is it going to take to show them the four photographs and ask them those questions?

David: I figure about twenty minutes in total.

Angela: Then what? The class is how long?

David: Eighty minutes. After we've talked about some of the issues, I'll put students in groups of four and give each group one book that I signed out of the library. I'll give them twenty minutes to browse through the book, looking at photographs, maps, or whatever, but mostly the photographs.

Angela: What do you expect them to do?

David: I'll ask each group to select one photograph and have them complete a worksheet. Then they will present their findings to the rest of the class. Wait a second, maybe I'll give them a blank overhead instead and ask each group to present their group's findings that way.

Angela: I think they're going to need clearer instructions than that. How much time are you going to give them to complete the worksheet?

David: Ten minutes. That means twenty minutes to browse through the book, and an additional ten minutes to do the overhead. I'll have to think through what I want them to present to the rest of the class, but they'll only have about ten minutes.

Angela: How many students are in this class?

David: Twenty-seven students. That means six groups of four, and one group of three. That's assuming that everyone is present. Oh no! There won't be enough time for each group to present their findings. I need to think about the timing of the lesson a little bit more.

Four days later, David walked down the hall to his History 12 class. He was really excited about this lesson. He felt confident that he had done everything necessary to ensure that it would be a very good lesson. He was satisfied that he had given enough thought to his students' prior knowledge and their individual abilities. He had also thought about how this lesson fits into the previous week's work. He was satisfied with the sequencing of the lesson, he knew he had interesting photographs and good books to share with his students, and he had thought about and written down specific questions he planned to ask students. David couldn't wait for the lesson to begin. The one area that he knew he still needed to think about was assessment and evaluation.

"Hello everyone!" David said as he entered his class.

"Nice clothes Mr. Pang! Cool earring!" they exclaimed.

GENERAL REFERENCES

Cruickshank, D., Bainer, D., & Metcalf, K. (1995). Planning instruction. In *The act of teaching* (pp. 127–162). New York: McGraw-Hill.

Lang, H., McBeath, A., & Hebert, J. (1995). Planning for teaching. In *Teaching: Strategies and methods for student-centered instruction* (pp. 51–78). Toronto: Harcourt Brace.

Ornstein, A. (1990). Instructional objectives. In *Strategies for effective teaching* (pp. 211–261). New York: HarperCollins.

SPECIFIC REFERENCES

Hirsch, E. (1989). *A first dictionary of cultural literacy: What our children need to know.* Boston: Houghton Mifflin.

Kirman, J. (1992). Using newspapers to study media bias. *Social Education, 56*(1), 47–51.

Shulman, L. (1987). Knowledge and teaching: Foundations of a new reform. *Harvard Educational Review, 57*(1), 1–22.

INSTRUCTIONAL STRATEGIES

FRACTIONS AND PEPPERONI:
Encouraging Students' Active Participation

"Mom, I need two dollars for pizza," Suria said to his mother as they were ready to leave for school. "We're going to study fractons all this week."

"Fractons?" Mrs. Dalliwhal looked at her son, unsure what he meant by "fractons."

"Yup, fractons or something. That's why I need money for pizza," he confirmed. "We're going to have a party so we can learn fractons. That's what Ms Luciani said."

Mrs. Dalliwhal reached for her purse and gave Suria two shining coins. It must be another one of Ms Luciani's innovations, she thought. She had no idea what "fractons" might be or how they could relate to a pizza lunch, but she liked her son's teacher and had confidence in her ability and judgment.

"Here Mom, I've got a note about it from Ms Luciani." Suria pulled a crumpled piece of paper from his backpack.

"Thanks Suria, but you should have given this to me last night. I don't have time now to read it. Let's go. You'll be late for school."

Erminia Luciani was a new teacher at Kerrington Elementary, a small K–4 school with an enrollment of just under 250 students. The school building, too small because of the area's growing population, is now surrounded by a row of portable classrooms. Like all new teachers at Kerrington, Erminia is teaching in a portable. The portable that Erminia inherited from Mr. Burgs is old, the carpet in one area is marked with large stains of red paint, and the air is heavy with a mouldy smell. However, Erminia is glad to have a space of her own, a place where she can try her approaches to teaching without the annoying interference of other teachers.

Last year at Fallbrook Elementary, the constant feeling of having her professional judgments questioned and needing to explain everything to the two other teachers who worked in the open-area classroom where Erminia was teaching made her so miserable that she requested a transfer. Her district superintendent had been sympathetic to her request and she was transferred to Kerrington Elementary. The school had a good reputation, and many of its teachers were of "the new generation" of educators. Erminia was hopeful that her more active, hands-on approach would be better accepted in this environment. She felt reassured by having her classroom separated from the main building. She wanted to create her own educational environment for her students, her own special world of learning.

Not that she didn't like to share her ideas with others. In fact, it was her eagerness to share that got her into trouble at Fallbrook Elementary last year. While she knew better than to generalize one negative experience with a handful of professional colleagues to the whole educational system in the province, she longed for the freedom to realize her own dream as a teacher and was dedicated to pursuing this goal.

It looked like this year was going to make this dream come true. From the first day of classes, Erminia fell in love with her kids. The 24 third graders in her charge seemed bright and enthusiastic about learning. Although they varied greatly in their abilities and some of her students seemed behind in their reading and writing skills, Erminia was confident that she would find ways to reach them all and accommodate their special needs.

The key to her strategy was an approach she had learned during her teacher education program, an approach that emphasized the active participation of learners. In her university courses Erminia was often complimented for her ability to combine different instructional strategies in her planning of lessons and units and for her emphasis on active student involvement. Her practicum experience confirmed that she was well able to put theory into practice. She would never forget the final words of her sponsor teacher: "You will be a wonderful teacher, Erminia! You have what it takes to make children learn and fully enjoy every minute of it."

The first snowflakes of the year were falling on the stairs as she entered her portable. She looked forward to the day ahead. As always when she was about to introduce a new concept to her students, she felt energetic and excited. She sometimes wondered if this joyous anticipation would eventually diminish after years of teaching experience. She opened the door and peered into the darkness. Erminia switched the lights on and looked around. She was pleased to see that the janitor had not moved anything last night. The classroom was set and ready for children to arrive, just the way she left it.

A large chart entitled "Fractions" was hanging by the carpeted area and the chalkboard was covered with colourful drawings that Erminia had drawn last night with her "magic chalk" and the carefully printed words "whole," "half," and "quarter." Erminia wondered if she should introduce other divisions right away, but decided against it. She wanted first to make sure that the children grasped the general notion of breaking a whole into sections before making things too complicated.

On each child's desk was a large envelope with big letters on the front. "Fractions Surprise. Do not open!!!" Erminia loved the excitement in her students' eyes whenever she made them wait to open "surprise packages." It seemed that these surprise packets could help make even the most boring concepts interesting.

As the children began to arrive, Erminia greeted them at the door, reminding them of the morning routine. "Did you bring your own book or do you want to take one from our library shelf?" She liked to offer her students a choice whenever possible. When the bell rang, most of the children were already seated on the carpet, reading or looking over illustrations in their books.

Erminia sat among them and began with a brief overview of the day's agenda. "Who remembers the special topic of the day?"

she asked. A forest of raised hands grew in front of her eyes. "Suria?" she said, calling on a little boy who had just recently, after much encouragement, learned to overcome his shyness in group activities. English was a second language for Suria, whose family immigrated from India just four years ago, and Erminia was glad to see him more comfortable speaking in front of the group.

"Fractons," Suria replied with a smile.

"Good try Suria. Close, but not quite." She smiled gently as she turned to Betty. "Betty, could you try to answer my question, please?"

"Fractions," Betty replied in a small voice.

"Very good. Can you try to put your answer into a whole sentence, Betty?"

"The topic for the day is fractions," Betty replied.

"Thank you, Betty. Good job!" Erminia praised the little girl for her attempt to overcome her habit of giving one-word responses.

Erminia got up and stood in front of the chart. Speaking slowly and clearly, she began to explain the concept of fractions, checking frequently for students' understanding. She called different students to come up and point to halves and quarters of a whole and to match them with the correct mathematical notations. When she was satisfied that all of her students had a basic understanding of the concept, she directed them to move toward their desks.

"Do not open your envelopes before the go-ahead signal," she reminded her students. "You will be working in pairs," she announced. "Who can quickly tell me some important things we should keep in mind when working with a partner?" Again, several children raised their hands and responded:

"Not to speak at once."

"Take turns."

"Be encouraging."

Erminia was reassured that they were ready to begin. She had introduced cooperative working skills early in the year but was careful not to take them for granted.

With desks arranged in sets of two, Erminia directed children to work with the person sitting next to them. "The person sitting on my right hand will choose which envelope we will open today," she announced, holding her right hand up. "The person on my left will take out the contents of the envelope." Erminia changed her hands. "Can I see all the people who will choose the envelopes raise their hands, please? Good, very good. Josh and Crystal," she addressed a pair who seemed to be undecided, "which one of you is sitting on my right-hand side?" Erminia leaned to the right to emphasize direction.

"I am," answered Crystal.

"Very well then, you are the one to select the envelope." Now she was ready to give the go-ahead sign. As children hastily opened the packages, Erminia gave them some time to inspect the contents. "What do you think we will do with these pieces of paper?" she asked. Two hands went up instantly. She waited a bit longer to encourage other students to seek the answer and then called on Rodney, one of the best students in the class. She knew that the boy must be eager to share his answer with others. She was pleased that Rodney was learning to let other children speak up as well, but she knew that she had to give him numerous occasions to participate in order to keep him engaged and happy.

"We are going to put pieces together to make whole shapes!" Rodney exclaimed.

"Excellent, Rodney. You are reading my mind! And what do you think, Cheng Shiang?" She called on a tall girl sitting in the back row who was holding her hand up. The girl hesitated. "Take your time Cheng Shiang, a good answer sometimes takes time to figure out."

"We, we will put them away at the clean-up time?"

"Yes, you are right, we will need to do a clean-up after we finish the assignment."

Erminia demonstrated how to use the manipulatives and then asked each team to get to work. She circulated around the class to monitor the children's work and offer help where needed. After a while, she had the children report on their progress. Each team reported on how many full circles and full squares they were able to put together, and how many halves and how many quarters were needed to complete the assignment. She recorded their answers on a large chart. Then she directed her students to put the pieces back in the envelopes.

Erminia glanced at her watch. "Well, we have just enough time before recess to play the 'wholes and halves' game," she declared. "Listen carefully to my questions and raise your hand when you know the answer. This time everyone is on his or her own. Take your time, but try to come up with an answer. I want everyone to think really hard. Are you ready?" Erminia pulled three celery sticks out of a large grocery bag. "How many pieces will I have if I cut each of these celery sticks in half?" she asked. About half of her students raised their hands right away. "Let's wait for everyone to have a chance to think about the answer." When almost everyone's hand was up, she called on one of her students.

"Six pieces," said Tamara.

"Tamara says that we will have six pieces. Who agrees with Tamara?" Erminia noticed many of her students waving their hands. "Who would like to propose a different answer? No one? Well, excellent. You are all right. Let's try another question." This time she pulled out of her bag six chocolate bars.

"Twelve pieces!" shouted Rodney before Erminia had a chance to pose her question.

"Well Rodney, your answer would have been right if my question had to do with halves. I am glad that you are so quick in your thinking, but you should first listen to the question and then raise your hand, okay? Is everyone ready? How many pieces will I have if I cut each bar into quarters?" Rodney's hand was the first one up. Erminia made eye contact with him and, while waiting for the other children to figure out the answer, approached Rodney, put her hand on his shoulder, and spoke softly. "I know you know the answer, Rodney. But I also want to make sure that everyone else can solve this problem. You understand, right?" Rodney nodded his head in agreement, pleased with being recognized. "All right. Sabrina?"

"24 pieces," Sabrina stated.

"Can you explain to me how you came up with your answer?" Erminia asked.

"Each bar has four quarters and you have six bars, so I just kept on adding the pieces," Sabrina replied.

"Very good, has everyone heard the answer? Sabrina noted that there are four quarters in each candy bar, so she added six groups of four together. Very good, Sabrina, good strategy!" Erminia checked her watch again. "The bell will ring any minute, and we still have one more thing to do. Did everyone remember to bring two dollars for our pizza party? I would like you now to get the money and put it on your desk. But please do it quietly as I have a very important job to do and I can't do it right if there is too much noise."

"What job, Ms Luciani?" Rodney asked. Erminia smiled. She could always count on Rodney's curiosity. "Well, since the class correctly calculated that six chocolate bars divided into quarters make 24 pieces, I just thought ..."

"Oh, I know, I know!" Kelly called from the back of the room. Kelly was a bit of a mystery to Erminia. Often it seemed that she was daydreaming rather than listening to class discussions, but when questions were asked she always knew the answer.

"Yes Kelly?"

"There are 24 of us!" Kelly exclaimed.

"You are absolutely right. I am about to prepare for you a little recess treat, but I can't cut the bars into equal pieces if you do not keep quiet." It's working, Erminia thought, dividing the candy bars and watching children quietly prepare the pizza money.

Just then the bell rang. "Please stay in your seats. I will walk around and collect your money. As soon as you give me your coins, you can come up to my desk and help yourself to a piece of chocolate bar. Just remember, one piece each. We only have 24 quarters," she added. Erminia posed one last question before beginning her tour of the classroom. "What is it that we were learning about today? Herman, can you tell us please?"

"We talked about halves and quarters," Herman replied.

"Very good!"

"Suria, do you remember the word that you got almost right this morning? We were learning today about …"

"Fractions," said Suria, finishing the sentence without hesitation.

"Great job!" Erminia praised him, smiling as she began to move around the classroom collecting money to pay for the tasty "manipulatives" for her next lesson about fractions.

GENERAL REFERENCES

Eggen, P., & Kauchack, D. (1996).The integrative model. In *Strategies for teachers: Teaching content and thinking skills* (2nd ed.) (pp. 180–204). Toronto: Allyn & Bacon.

Freiberg, H., & Driscoll, A. (1996). Interactive practice for learning: Beyond drill. In *Universal teaching strategies* (2nd ed.) (pp. 231–260). Toronto: Allyn & Bacon.

Lang, H., McBeath, A., & Herbert, J. (1995). Interactive and experiential instructional strategies. In *Teaching: Strategies and methods for student-centered instruction* (pp. 291–313). Toronto: Harcourt Brace.

SPECIFIC REFERENCES

Burchfield, D. (1996). Teaching all children: Four developmentally appropriate curricular and instructional strategies in primary-grade classrooms. *Young Children, 52*(1), 4–10.

Kohn, A. (1996). What to look for in a classroom. *Educational Leadership, 54*(1), 54–55.

Renne, C. (1996). Structuring classroom lessons: Attempts to incorporate student questions and initiatives during math lessons. *Teacher Education Quarterly, 23*(2), 5–18.

COOPERATIVE LEARNING EXPERIMENT: Positive Interdependence and Individual Accountability

The novel study was almost completed. Angela Dragut, a grade 7 teacher at Discovery Elementary School, was arranging folders containing her students' work on her desk. She was pleased with the progress of this language arts unit: most of her students did really well on the written assignments, and they seemed interested in the project. Angela was glad that, instead of assigning the same book for all of her students to read, she gave them a choice of several novels, all having to do with the issue of survival. At first she was concerned that some students would take forever to make their selection. However, with the exception of Troy, Dominique, and Chai, who never seemed to be able to make up their minds about anything, the class moved right along with the assignment after they had glanced over the brief summaries of each novel that Angela had prepared for them. While some titles were more popular than others — with *Lost in the Barrens* and *The Upstairs Room* attracting the most attention — each novel was read by at least three students.

This gave Angela the idea to structure the final assignment of the unit as a cooperative learning activity. She had not tried this strategy with her students before, but she heard a lot about it and wanted to give it a try. She thought that a group project would help underachieving students improve their marks. Angela was delighted that Lisa, Amber, Klaus, and Travis, who had barely been passing the assignments so far, all selected novels that some of her strongest students had also chosen. She consulted her class list again to make sure that she could successfully form groups of students with mixed abilities. "Yes, it will work just fine," she thought, pleased to have confirmed her prediction.

Angela decided to ask her students to invent a board game related to the events in their novels. This should be a perfect cooperative learning activity, she thought. They will have a chance to review the content of the novel together, select events and characters to be represented in the game, design the structure and rules of the game, and make decisions about the visual representation of their ideas. With a project that involved both thinking and doing and planning and executing, Angela was reassured that every student would be able to build on his or her strengths.

When she mentioned the project to the students, her idea was received with excitement. "This is going to be great," Pawel commented. "Finally we are going to do something really creative!" Pawel was one of the best students in the class. He tended to complete all his work ahead of time and to standards that exceeded Angela's expectations. He also, without being asked, illustrated his reports with magnificent drawings.

"A game? What kind of a game?" asked Rachel, who always wanted to have everything explained to her in the greatest detail.

"Any kind of board game that you wish," Angela replied. "The only requirement is that you use some sort of a board and that the game have to do with the novel that you selected for the survival novel study unit. Is that clear now?"

"So who is going to work with whom?" Hillel inquired.

"Tara, Lien Chun, and I will work together," Hana announced. She noted Akeo, Roman, John, and Harumi pulling their desks together before she had a chance to instruct her students to move into groups.

"Wait a minute. We have to make sure that all the people in each group have read the same novel," she tried to remind her students. She knew that Akeo's reading selection was different from that of Roman, John, and Harumi.

"But I want to work with this group," Akeo insisted. "Maybe I didn't choose *Lost in the Barrens* for the novel study but I read it a while ago and I know it pretty well."

"No Akeo, you are going to work with people who studied *The Upstairs Room*, just like you." Angela was not about to give up.

"What a drag," she heard Akeo comment as he reluctantly moved across the room to join Elsa, Brigitte, Dominique, Elizabeth, Karl, Saroj, and Prabha.

"There are too many of you in this group. You need to split into two teams," Angela prompted them. "Organize yourselves so that you have three to four people in each group, OK?" she said to the whole class.

"Can't be done," Allister noted. "There are five of us who read *Hunter in the Dark*, so either we stay together or one group will be very small."

Angela hesitated, then said: "Well, why don't you five decide what you want to do. Either way will be fine with me."

"But it won't be fair, Ms Dragut," Hana remarked. "If they all work together, each will have much less to do than we will. There are only three people in my group."

"Come on, Hana, this really is not an issue," said Angela, trying to change the focus of the conversation. "Why won't you just get to work and try to enjoy this project?"

Turning around, she noted that Amber was sitting all alone at her desk. "Amber, which group will you be working with?" Instead of a response, Amber gave her a puzzled look. Amber had been a problem throughout the term. Her English was not very good, and, to make matters worse, she was extremely shy. She had been in Canada for just over a year, and, despite some well-meant efforts by several girls in the class, she did not seem to have made any friends. Amber's academic performance was not very impressive, and Angela wondered if Amber ever really tried to improve her academic standing. She seemed ambivalent to everything that was going on in the classroom and did not appear to be affected in any way by her poor marks. Or if she was, she never showed any emotion.

"Amber, why don't you join Hana's group?" Angela proposed. Her suggestion was met with a look of disapproval from the group.

Lien Chun expressed the sentiment of the group: "We already have a group all formed and we know what we're doing. We all live close to each other, so we can do some work after school. Maybe Amber can work with somebody else." Angela knew that Hana, Lien Chun, and Tara were good friends and she was not surprised to see them try to defend the privacy of their group.

"Well, Lien Chun, Amber read the same book as you and she needs some people to work with. Please make her feel welcome," Angela suggested.

"Sure, you can join us Amber," came Tara's response, the tone of her voice contradicting the invitation.

"Well, at least we have the group assignments settled," Angela concluded, looking at her watch. "Goodness, it took us so much time. I'm afraid you will need to start working on this project for homework. By tomorrow, I expect you to have figured out a general idea of the game and to have begun working on it. We will then finish the project in class. Is that clear?" Just about then the bell rang. "Tomorrow please don't forget to bring any materials you might need to work on your game, " she reminded her students as they rushed out.

"Ms Dragut, we have a problem," Prabha said as he approached her desk. "Hillel has a cello practice this afternoon and Elsa promised her neighbour that she would baby-sit, so there is no time we can all meet after school."

"Well, just do your best. You can use the phone too to discuss your plans," Angela suggested. It was really too bad that they ran out of time and didn't get a chance to discuss their games in class. "Perhaps I should have waited till tomorrow to have them begin the project," Angela wondered. "Anyway, it's too late now — I already assigned the homework."

The next morning, when Angela entered the classroom, she noted her students crowding around Pawel's desk. "Ms Dragut, look at this! Pawel did such a good job," Saroj exclaimed. As she leaned over Akeo's shoulder, Angela saw a large square of laminated board, with beautifully rendered game paths. The game pieces were modelled in Plasticine with amazing detail. Next to the board were two stacks of small cards containing questions and answers that were to be used to move the players along. It was obvious that the game was absolutely perfect. Once again, Pawel had displayed his amazing talent.

Everyone in class was impressed, and Pawel was beaming with satisfaction. "Do you like it, Ms Dragut?" he asked.

"Yes, it is very nice, Pawel, but you were supposed to work on this project with some of your classmates," Angela said.

"Oh, I did!" Pawel reassured her. " I talked about it with Rachel and Troy on the phone last night."

"Yes, we did discuss it," Rachel confirmed. "It was my suggestion to put the question and answer cards on the side. Pawel initially wanted them all to fit on the board."

Troy added: "And I gave the idea to make the game pieces out of Plasticine. I even bought the Plasticine and brought it to Pawel's."

"But Pawel did all the work, didn't he?" asked Angela.

"You never said how we should divide the work," commented Rachel.

"Do you think, Rachel, that it is fair to expect Pawel to do all this work and for the three of you to get a mark for it?" said

Angela, trying to appeal to Rachel's sense of fairness.

"That's fine with me," Pawel responded. "Rachel and Troy offered to help, but it was easier for me to do it myself. I don't have any problems with everyone getting a good mark," he concluded. "This deserves a good mark, doesn't it?"

"Well, Pawel, I'll need to think about it," said Angela. She wasn't sure what she should do. She never expected any of the teams to bring the finished project the very next day. "How did Pawel manage to do all this work in one afternoon, anyway?" she wondered.

As if reading her mind, Pawel answered: "I stayed up almost all night to finish this game. It took a lot of time and a lot of effort. Are you saying that I did it for nothing?"

"No, Pawel, I certainly appreciate what you did," said Angela, "but this was supposed to be a group project with everyone contributing an equal share."

"But Ms Dragut, you never told us how we were supposed to work on this project," Allister said, offering Pawel his support.

"That's true," Roman added. "Pawel and his team should not be penalized for doing too good a job too quickly."

Angela felt that she was losing ground. How did she get herself into this mess? What should she do now? As confused as she was at the moment, one thing was certain for Angela: she truly regretted her cooperative learning experiment. "Never again," she thought, as she struggled to find an immediate solution to her problem.

GENERAL REFERENCES

Kagan, S. (1994). *Cooperative learning.* San Juan, Cappiatrano, CA: Kagan Cooperative Learning.

Ornstein, A. (1990). Grouping for instruction. In *Strategies for effective teaching* (pp. 399–462). New York: HarperColllins.

Putnam, J. (1997). *Cooperative learning in diverse classrooms.* Upper Saddle River: Prentice-Hall.

SPECIFIC REFERENCES

Abrami, R., Chambers, B., Poulsen, C., Simone, C., D'Apollonia, S., & Howden, J. (1995). Group project methods. In *Classrooms connections: Understanding and using cooperative learning* (pp. 157–165). Toronto: Harcourt Brace.

Putnam, J. (1997). Assessment in cooperative learning. In *Cooperative learning in diverse classrooms* (pp. 177–193). Upper Saddle River: Prentice-Hall.

Roy, P., & Hoch, J. (1994). Cooperative learning: A principal's perspective. *Principal, 73*(4), 27–29.

JUSTIFY YOUR LESSON: Reflecting on Choices in Teaching Strategies

13

"I want to thank you for your hard work and cooperation in your groups today," Harjeet Bains said to his Humanities 8 class. "You posed interesting questions, and I look forward to reading your answers. Your homework is to continue reading the novel up to at least Chapter 5. You will also need to complete another journal entry for next class. Before the bell rings, I need everyone to help me rearrange the desks into a horseshoe the way Mr. Weston organizes the room." With much scraping and bumping, the desks were reconfigured and Harjeet's class was dismissed.

Harjeet sighed: "Prep block! Now I can get started reading over their work."

"Let's take a look at what they did," responded Ray Weston, Harjeet's sponsor teacher, who had been working at the computer in the back corner of the room for the past hour. "I'm curious to see what the stu-

dents came up with. I hope they addressed the main issues and events of the novel. The students might miss key points if allowed to create the questions and then choose which few to answer. Why did you decide to do it that way?"

Harjeet studied Ray, wondering if this was a sincere question or a covert critique of his teaching. Still, Ray seemed genuinely interested. During this first month of the extended practicum at Mariner Lane Middle School, Ray had given Harjeet a lot of freedom to try out different strategies, even when they involved rearranging the room. Harjeet tried to collect his thoughts so that he could explain his teaching methods to his sponsor teacher.

The past hour replayed itself in Harjeet's mind:

I moved the desks into groups and turned to the door to greet the students as they arrived. "Hi Nadine and Kim. You two look out of breath. What were you up to at lunch?"

"Volleyball. We beat green house!" Kim exuberantly replied.

"Hey, Mr. Bains," Nadine interjected, looking at the groups of desks around the room, "where do we sit?"

I pointed to the board where I had printed in large letters: "Sit in Your Groups (Same as Last Week)."

Just as the bell rang to begin the class, Ray, my sponsor teacher, slipped into the room to use the computer, and I began the lesson I'd spent the weekend planning. "Please take out your journals that we began last week." I paused until the rustle of papers subsided. "You each should now have three entries in your journal and in each of those entries you have posed questions about the novel. Your questions will be the focus of this lesson. In your base groups, you will have ten minutes to make one list of all the questions your group members posed in their journals. The recorder for this activity will be group member B."

As the students began reading and recording their questions, I circulated among the groups to assess what types of questions they had posed and to encourage them to stay on task. The room hummed with voices. After about ten minutes, I returned to the front of the room and called for attention.

"Before we look at your lists, I'm going to show you three types of questions." I then wrote on the board three questions about the novel and asked the students what the difference was between them. The students were able to determine that the first question could be answered by just looking in the book while the second one could be figured out by using clues in the book. The third question, however, required students to use information that was already in their heads. I explained that the "in your head" questions would be the ones that they would

consider this class. "In your groups, decide which of the questions on your list are 'in your head' questions. Group member C will put a star by these questions." I remembered to pause to allow the students to process my instructions.

While the students worked, I divided the board into four sections, which I labelled "Chapter 1," "Chapter 2," "Chapter 3," and "General." The rising noise level told me that the students were finished, so I assigned the D's in each group to write the starred questions on the appropriate sections of the board. The rest of the group members were to read the questions that their peers were putting on the board and choose one from each section for their group to answer. When all the questions were on the board, I told the A's to put their group number by the questions their group had chosen. "Remember, only one group can do each question, so if your first choice is already picked, make another choice." The A's enthusiastically rushed to the board, and within a minute the choices had been made and the students were seated once again in their groups.

I told them that they would have the remaining 25 minutes of the class to answer the four questions they had chosen in their groups. "At the end of the class, each group will hand in one page with the four answers written below the four questions. The role of recorder will switch for each question. For example, in group three, Lee, Benson, Nadine, and Jenny will each be responsible for recording their group's response to one of their chosen questions. I reminded them to work together to answer the questions.

The students were really involved in this activity. They were thinking, talking, debating. When I collected their answers, I was pleased with how much they had written. Some of their answers were more legible than others; nevertheless, they had accomplished a lot.

Harjeet looked up at Ray, who was still waiting for his response, and said: "What you're asking for is my rationale, right?"

Ray nodded.

GENERAL REFERENCES

Eggen, P., & Kauchack, D. (1996). Developing thinking skills through inquiry. In *Strategies for teachers: Teaching content and thinking skills* (2nd ed.) (pp. 235–275). Toronto: Allyn & Bacon.

Freiberg, H., & Driscoll, A. (1996). Reflective teaching and learning: Students as shareholders. In *Universal teaching strategies* (2nd ed.) (pp. 293–320). Toronto: Allyn & Bacon.

Lang, H., McBeath, A., & Herbert, J. (1995). Asking and answering questions. In *Teaching: Strategies and methods for student-centered instruction* (pp. 153–171). Toronto: Harcourt Brace.

SPECIFIC REFERENCES

Brownlie, F., & Close, S. (1992). ReQuest. In *Beyond chalk and talk* (pp. 87–95). Markham, ON: Pembroke Publishing.

Kohn, A. (1996). What to look for in a classroom. *Educational Leadership, 54*(1), 54–55.

Rosenshine, B. (1996). Teaching students to generate questions: A review of intervention strategies. *Review of Educational Research, 66*(2), 181–221.

CHAOS OR COOPERATION:
Planning for Group Work

Allison Taylor grimaced at the weight of her book bag as she slung it over her shoulder. "Must be all those handouts from the conference," she muttered as she struggled to gain her balance and walk across the icy parking lot into McConachie Secondary. Allison had been teaching in this northern town since completing her education degree four years ago. She had only intended to teach at McConachie for a year or two, but had since made good friends, bought a house, and decided to stay in this resource-based community. Nevertheless, when Allison was offered the opportunity to attend a Science Educators Conference in the city where she had attended university, she was keen to head south for a few days. Now she was back with a binder full of teaching ideas, tired but enthusiastic after the two days at the conference and two days of travelling.

Allison made her way through the halls of McConachie Secondary, greeting stu-

dents as she passed. "Allison!" It was Thomas Lee, a math and physics teacher and one of her closest friends on staff. "So how was the big city?"

"Great!" said Allison. "It was good to connect with other science teachers, and some of the workshops were really practical. In fact, I'm trying out cooperative learning with my science nines first thing this morning. I haven't had much time to plan because I just got back last night, but it seems pretty straightforward: I put students in groups, they help each other do the assignment, and I have less marking to take home tonight!" Allison laughed. For Allison, cooperative learning had been a popular buzzword in education, but before attending this conference she had not considered how she might use cooperative strategies in her science classes.

Arriving at her classroom with fifteen minutes to spare before the bell, Allison eased her heavy bag onto the table at the front and picked up the note left for her from the teacher-on-call. "Good." she thought. "He covered the introductory section of chapter 5 on simple machines with the grade nines just as I had asked. I'm glad the class didn't fall behind, so I'll be able to get on with today's topic."

She was writing the agenda for the lesson on the overhead when the first bell rang and students began to arrive, taking their seats at the four long lab tables. Unlike her grade eights, Allison let the 28 students in this class sit wherever they liked because they were generally more mature and task-oriented. "Hey, Ms Taylor's back!" Josh announced. "How was the concert?"

Allison smiled, shook her head, and replied, "It was a conference not a concert. In fact, I brought back some good ideas that we are going to use today." The second bell rang. She switched on the overhead and addressed the whole class. "Good morning everyone. I'm back, and we have lots of work to do today. Please pass your homework questions to the left so that I can collect them, and then take a look at the agenda on the overhead." A few students groaned, although they were used to this procedure. "First I am going to ask you some questions to see what you learned while I was away. Then I have just a few notes on levers for you to copy. And for your assignment today, we are going to try something different, which I'll tell you about after we finish the review and notes."

The first twenty minutes of the class went smoothly. By asking a question, waiting a few seconds, and then calling on random students, Allison was able to determine that the students had understood the material on simple machines covered by the teacher-on-call. She also used her usual strategy for giving notes: she explained a point and then uncovered that point in the notes on the overhead, allowing students to finish writing before moving on to the next point. The students were so quiet and cooperative during the notetaking that Allison wondered if they weren't still asleep. "Well I'll wake them up with this group activity," she mused.

"For today's activity, we will be doing something different. You will be working with the people at your table to complete Activity 5.6 on page 103 of your textbook, but instead of each person writing out the lab, each group will work cooperatively to complete one write-up. Does anyone have any questions?"

"Ms Taylor, do I have to work in a group?" complained Asha, a serious and hard-working student. "I'd rather just do it myself." Asha's comment caused a ripple of responses throughout the room. Some students agreed that they wanted to work alone, yet most argued that group work meant less work.

"Hold on!" called Allison, gaining the students' attention once again. "Everyone will work in groups. Group cooperation is an important skill. Now stop wasting time and get to work. I'll put some metre sticks, weights, spring scales, and tin cans on the demonstration table for you to pick up. Remember to work together with the five other people at your table. The activity will be handed in for ten marks at the end of class."

Allison had barely finished giving directions when students rushed up to collect supplies. "One of each per group!" she reminded them over the noise. The students settled in their seats along the long tables while Allison silently checked attendance and scanned through the stack of homework questions until the steadily escalating noise of the class caused her to look up. She was beginning to wonder if she had given this lesson enough thought. The group at the back table were arguing over who would write up the lab. As Allison made her way to the back, she noticed that Asha was setting up the lever by herself, leaving three of her group members to chat about the upcoming dance and the other two members to work on French homework. In fact, very few of the students in this usually mature and hard-working class were on task at all! In a state of panic, Allison checked the clock. "Five minutes left to finish and hand this in!"

Sounds of protest rose from around the room. "There's not enough time," complained Josh.

Asha raised her hand. "Ms Taylor, can I finish this for homework?"

"Should I let those who actually experimented with the levers write up their lab on their own at home?" thought Allison. "Or should I spend more time on this activity than I planned and give them time next class to complete the work in groups? Either way, I've learned that while cooperative learning sounds good in theory, it sure doesn't work with my students."

GENERAL REFERENCES

Arends, R. (1994). Cooperative learning. In *Learning to teach* (pp. 339–356). New York: McGraw Hill.

Eby, J., & Kujawa, E. (1994). Cooperative learning strategies. In *Reflective planning, teaching, and evaluation: K–12* (pp. 205–224). Toronto: Macmillan.

Eggen, P., & Kauchack, D. (1996). The cooperative learning model. In *Strategies for teachers: Teaching content and thinking skills* (2nd ed.) (pp. 276–312). Toronto: Allyn & Bacon.

SPECIFIC REFERENCES

Abrami, R., Chambers, B., Poulsen, C., Simone, C., D'Apollonia, S., & Howden, J. (1995). Learning together. In *Classroom connections: Understanding and using cooperative learning* (pp.149–156). Toronto: Harcourt Brace.

Roy, P., & Hoch, J. (1994). Cooperative learning: A principal's perspective. *Principal, 73*(4), 27–29.

Strong, R., Silver, H., & Robinson, A. (1995). What do students want? *Educational Leadership, 53*(1), 8–12.

NET WORTH:
Computers in the Classroom

Jason Urfano, a visual arts student-teacher, was four weeks into his extended practicum at Meadow Valley Secondary School, a large suburban high school. Since completing his Bachelor of Fine Arts with a concentration in painting three years ago, Jason has exhibited several of his works in several small galleries. As a student teacher, he is sharing his interest in art with high-school students.

Jason took a deep breath and walked into his classroom. He was really enjoying his practicum placement and he was doubly excited about the lesson he was about to begin with his grade 12 art class. "Good afternoon everyone, I hope you had a great weekend. I told you last class that we're going to do something a little different today. That's why I arranged to have our class in this computer lab." Jason looked around the room and was pleased that only one student was absent. He really wanted this lesson to go well.

"The purpose of the next few lessons," Jason continued, "is for you to explore the travelling exhibit of Impressionist paintings, 1850–1900, at the Art Gallery of Ontario (AGO) in Toronto. I want you to use this website." Jason drew his students' attention to the address he had written on the blackboard. "Over the next few classes, you will tour the exhibit, and post your reactions to the paintings on a website forum. Art students in Ottawa will do the same thing."

"I should tell you," Jason pointed out, "that it was Ms Crandall, the Art Department Head, not I, who set up this website forum. We're lucky to have the opportunity to study the AGO exhibit."

Jason continued: "First, after you log on, select Main Collections, then Special Exhibit. From there, you will be able to access approximately 120 paintings. For each painting, you will see comments from the students in Ottawa. I want each person in the group to examine the paintings, and also to comment about what you think.

"Let me remind everyone about the school's policy for the Internet. No inappropriate language or comments, and do not leave this website. Is that clear? Any questions?

"The project you will begin today will take two weeks; it's a project based on Impressionist painting. I want you to focus," Jason emphasized, "on colour and light theory." One of Jason's objectives was to link Impressionist paintings to some of the scientific discoveries of the day such as the camera and the development of lenses and prisms.

Jason raised his voice a little, signalling to his students that he wanted them to be extra attentive. "I want you all to be clear about what I expect before you begin." Jason turned on the overhead projector, revealing a neatly typed overview of upcoming lessons. He found that his students produced better work when he made everything explicit to them. Under "Objectives," Jason expected each student to investigate one Impressionist painter, including things like biographical information, painting techniques, and media, as well as to provide their personal reactions to the work. Jason explained to the whole class that he expected each person to work on the project outside of class time, and that the computer lab was available before and after school.

One of the features of the lessons that Jason was most excited about was that students would be able to post their finished projects on the website forum that had been established by his school district, in cooperation with the Ottawa Board of Education and the AGO. At first, Jason was a little intimidated at the prospect of using the Internet in this fashion, but his apprehen-sion was relieved after he talked to Allan, the technical support person at Meadow Valley. Allan assured Jason that he would be available if anything went wrong.

Jason wanted to make sure that his students were clear about the different components of the project. "Each person," he said, "will be expected to write in their journal on a daily basis and to create outside sketches each week. These sketches might be helpful for future projects. Remember," Jason emphasized, "each person will produce a five-page research paper on an Impressionist artist."

Jason noticed that some of his students were itching to begin, so he quickly pressed on. "At the end of the project, each person will make a brief presentation to the rest of the class." Jason pointed to item 2 on the overhead under evaluation. "Each person will also be responsible for completing a personal critique sheet. You've done these before, so this isn't anything new."

Jason was finding it a little difficult to maintain his students' attention at this point. "One more thing before you begin: I want you to think about and write down a list of your successes and failures when doing this project. For example, what went well, what problems you encountered. Things like that, okay?" Jason told his class that they could begin.

It didn't take long for the first problem to surface. A collective groan could be heard from his students. "Mr. Urfano, something is wrong with this computer," one of them said. Jason hurried to assist those students who were having difficulty logging on.

"Hold on everyone. Stop what you're doing and listen. It looks like some of you are unable to log on. Let's wait a few minutes, and then try again, okay?"

After a few false starts, all of the students were connected to the website. At 3 p.m., Jason announced that only ten minutes were left in the period and that everyone should prepare to shut off the computers. He would see everyone on Wednesday.

After all his students had left for the day, Sheila, a fellow visual arts student-teacher, entered Jason's room. "How did it go?" she asked.

"At least my sponsor teacher wasn't here to witness what happened," replied Jason. "Let's just say that it didn't go as well as I would have liked. Technology is a wonderful thing when it works, but it's a real pain when it breaks down."

What happened?" asked Sheila. Jason wasn't sure where to start. "What was the website like?" Sheila persisted. Jason didn't know as much about the website as he would have liked, but nevertheless he attempted to explain to Sheila.

"The collection was set up by the Art Gallery of Ontario for school groups. When I looked at the website forum last weekend, there were a lot of really interesting and insightful comments made by the other students in Ottawa. I really enjoyed reading what they had to say about the exhibit."

"I'm with you so far," Sheila said, "but I don't see the problem yet." Sheila was puzzled why Jason was concerned about the lesson.

"Let me tell you what happened," continued Jason. "First of all, we had trouble logging on. It took almost half the period for some students to access the exhibit. I didn't know what to do with them while they tried to log on. Some of the other students already had questions and I felt like I was being pulled in two directions at once. I was a little frustrated. But that's only part of it. I can accept computer glitches, but what really troubles me is that one of my students, Graham, made this really inappropriate comment on the forum website."

"What did he say?" Sheila asked.

"He made a derogatory comment about Louise, another student in the class. He compared her body to an Impressionist nude painting by Gauguin, *The Spirit of the Dead Watching*. As well, I'm not sure whether or not Graham meant it as a racial slur. On top of everything else, I don't think Graham realized his comment was sent automatically to every student on the website. I don't pretend to understand exactly how it works, but apparently when a person makes a comment on the forum website, it's sent to everyone on the network. Allan, the support person, was unable to remove the comment. I feel really bad for Louise."

"What did you do with Graham?"

"Nothing at first," replied Jason. "I didn't notice the comment initially. It was only because I was helping another student that I stumbled across it by chance. That's what really bothers me. It's impossible to monitor this stuff. I'm not sure that the Internet is worth the trouble."

The next day, Jason was still thinking about the Internet lesson. On balance, he felt a certain amount of satisfaction from trying to use the Internet, even though it was a more complex and demanding task than he expected. He couldn't help but notice that most of his students actively participated and seemed to enjoy the opportunity of exploring the AGO's collection. Nevertheless, Jason wondered whether this type of activity was worth the trouble. And before the next class, Jason needed to figure out what to do with Graham.

GENERAL REFERENCES

Freiberg, H., & Driscoll, A. (1996). Using community resources, audiovisuals, computers and multimedia: Varying the stimuli. In *Universal teaching strategies* (2nd ed.) (pp. 345–376). Toronto: Allyn & Bacon.

Lang, H., McBeath, A., & Herbert, J. (1995). Individual study and instructional technology. In *Teaching: strategies and methods for student-centered instruction* (pp. 319–342). Toronto: Harcourt Brace.

Ornstein, A. (1990). Instructional technology. In *Strategies for effective teaching* (pp. 361–397). New York: HarperCollins.

SPECIFIC REFERENCES

Milheim, W. (1997). Instructional utilization of the Internet in public school settings. *Tech Trends, 42*(2), 19–23.

Owston, R. (1997). The World Wide Web: A technology to enhance teaching and learning? *Educational Researcher, 26*(2), 27–33.

ASSESSMENT, EVALUATION, AND REPORTING

Part IV

NICOLE'S NEW REPORT CARDS:
Making Decisions about Reporting

My friend, Nicole Darcy, completed her teacher education program two years ago and, after a few months of on-call teaching, settled in at Alliance Elementary School. Born in Montreal and proud of her French-Canadian heritage, Nicole feels fortunate to have the opportunity to teach in a French immersion school. French is a second language for all of the children in Nicole's grade 3 class, with the exception of Dominique, who is from a francophone family. Nicole is delighted to be working with primary children, the age group she enjoys the most. I have seen her teach on one or two occasions when I volunteered to help with special activities in her classroom and have a hard time believing that she is just a beginning teacher. She has a true gift for relating to young children in a way that creates an atmosphere of trust, respect, and fun in her classroom.

Mind you, Nicole has always been a high achiever, and she has excelled in her studies due as much to her hard work as to her enthusiasm and commitment to becoming a teacher. She never seemed to work "for marks," but, rather, for the satisfaction of doing the best job she can. Her willingness to accept a challenge was evident, once again, last week when we met for our monthly lunch on a Saturday afternoon.

As usual, Nicole arrived armed with her notebook, a thick red folder, and a large plastic bag. She was hoping to collect from me empty yogurt containers that she had asked me to save for her and that she was going to use as paint containers for her students. It was just like Nicole: her life really revolves around teaching!

After we agreed on what pizza to order, Nicole looked at me and said that she needed my advice. She had a problem that she was not sure how to solve and was hoping that I could help her decide on the best course of action.

The reporting period in her school was approaching, and Nicole was trying to decide how to respond to the problems that she noted the last time the report cards were sent home. The school policy required teachers to provide each student and his or her parents with a written commentary about the child's progress along with a photocopy of a sheet describing the main activities in which the students participated and a list of the broad learning objectives.

When Nicole was to prepare her report cards for the first time, Bernie, the vice-principal, provided her with a database of statements that could be cut and pasted in the reports. All of the teachers in the school were using the same database. Naturally, they were adding more personal comments, as needed, but for the most part the statements included in the file covered the range of global descriptors that one would use to describe a child's school performance.

At first, Nicole was skeptical about using such a database. She felt that the comments were not specific enough and did not convey the kind of information she would like to receive if she were a parent of one of her students. She was determined to write more personal, detailed reports for each of her kids. But it took her only one weekend to realize that her mission was impossible. After more than fourteen hours of work, she had written only five reports that she was pleased with. Each was several pages long and detailed the child's performance and growth in all areas of the curriculum and included comments about emotional and social development and work habits. There were simply not enough weekends left before the report cards had to be sent home, so Nicole reluctantly decided to follow the common practice of making only some general comments in her reports. She made sure to highlight any specific observations about students whose performance she was concerned about. However, reports of children who were generally successful included selected database statements about the student being "an enthusiastic and cooperative learner," "successfully achieving objectives

in grade 3 language arts," "demonstrating respect for others," and so on. While Nicole was not fully satisfied with her reports, she was glad that she managed to do them on time; besides, everyone in the school was doing the same.

However, her concerns about the reports were confirmed during the parent–teacher conferences, where she was consistently confronted with requests for more specificity. She remembered some of the parents saying that the reports contained information they already knew. "We know that our child is enthusiastic about learning and that she can read a simple story; she does it at home all the time," Nicole recalled them saying. Many complained that their children did not receive letter grades. Nicole's explanation that this practice was consistent with reporting guidelines for the primary program did not appease the parents. They were interested in knowing more about the competencies of their children both in comparison with the other children and in relation to established standards. As Nicole was trying to respond to these needs during the parent–teacher conferences, she soon realized that she was falling behind schedule and anxious parents were lining up outside of her classroom waiting for their appointments. Also, she found the process of extensive verbal reporting very exhausting. Something had to change.

When the first-term conferences were over, Nicole compiled a list of the most frequently asked questions and tried to come up with a checklist that she could integrate with her qualitative, descriptive report. In constructing her new reporting instrument, Nicole also used the progress report forms that her friend Kathleen had used in a French immersion school across town. It included items that were designed specifically to describe learning outcomes for grade 3 French immersion students. Nicole wanted me to have a look at a sample of her new report card.

When she put the report card on the table, I quickly recognized the quality of Nicole's work. Three pages of legal-size paper were divided into sections corresponding to the various areas of expected learning and growth. Each of the sections started with a paragraph or two describing the learning objectives in this area as well as ways in which the children were guided to achieve them through classroom activities. Beneath was an area left for comments, which was followed by a table listing specific learning outcomes (eight to fifteen, depending on the area) and a place to make a check mark in a column labelled 1, 2, or 3. A small legend on the top of the first sheet indicated that a check mark in column 1 meant that a child had successfully achieved the objectives, 2 was indicative of a satisfactory achievement, and 3 pointed to the need of further attention or development. Finally, at the bottom of the last page was ample space to write summary remarks.

When I told Nicole that I was impressed with her work and that I wished my children's teachers would use this reporting format, she was visibly pleased, but it seemed that my words only confirmed what she already knew. I was puzzled about what her problem could be. "You have done a great job Nicole," I assured her. "You'll see — the parents will be thrilled to see this change. What is it that bothers you?"

"It's not the parents I worry about," Nicole confessed. It turned out that she had shared her plans with a colleague in her school and her enthusiasm had been quickly undermined by the very cold reception of her idea. The following day she overheard another teacher making sarcastic comments about "a certain new teacher " who thinks that "she is better than everyone else" and comes up with ideas that will mean more work for everyone in the end. "I'm not sure if I have enough confidence to go ahead with this project now. I don't want to have

the rest of the teachers against me. So far I've had a really good relationship with my colleagues. I'm not sure what I should do." Nicole looked at me, expecting an answer.

"You should ask this question of people who are teachers," I replied. "They will be in the best position to give good advice. After all, I am just a friend."

GENERAL REFERENCES

Cornfield, R. (1987). *Making the grade: Evaluating student progress.* Etobicoke Board of Education. Scarborough, ON: Prentice-Hall.

Eby, J., & Kujawa, E. (1994). Two-way communication with parents. In *Reflective planning, teaching, and evaluation: K–12* (pp. 304–317). Toronto: Maxwell Macmillan.

SPECIFIC REFERENCES

Kenney, E., & Perry, S. (1994). Talking with parents about performance-based report cards. *Educational Leadership, 52*(2), 24–27.

Wiggins, G. (1994). Toward better report cards. *Educational Leadership, 52*(2), 28–37.

HALLOWEEN BOOKS:
What and How to Assess

"What's wrong? What are the students upset about?" Jenny Lee, a student-teacher at Prince Charles Elementary, wanted to ask Alex, her sponsor teacher. She has been on her extended practicum since September, and over the past two months has developed a good working relationship with Alex. She would usually ask him for advice in a situation like this, but, unfortunately, today Alex was at home sick with the flu.

While at the beginning of her practicum Jenny mostly assisted Alex, she has been gaining more independence in planning and delivering instruction to the 29 grade 6 and 7 children, who seem very responsive to her efforts. Her class of sixteen boys and thirteen girls of diverse cultural backgrounds seems to have bonded well as a group, and Alex has complimented Jenny on contributing to the positive atmosphere in the classroom. Jenny is feeling increasingly comfortable

with her role and is particularly pleased that she has had to face only minor management problems over the past few weeks. Jenny also believes that she has a good grasp on lesson planning, organizing class activities, and trying a variety of instructional strategies. She thinks that the students respond well to her teaching and enjoy the assignments that she carefully plans for them each day.

This Monday morning, Jenny walked into the classroom particularly pleased. She had finished marking the Halloween books that her students made for their reading buddies in Thalia's kindergarten class. She had asked the students to write a Halloween story, to illustrate it, and collate it into an attractive Halloween book. She had shown students a few Halloween books as examples that they could follow. The quality of the students' books had pleasantly surprised her. Their stories were imaginative and fun, and the drawings in some of the books exceeded her expectations. Last night, when she was marking this assignment, she tried very hard to ensure that the marks she was giving sufficiently differentiated between good and excellent work.

She gave the books back to the students shortly before the recess. As the students checked their marks and the brief comments that she attached to each book, Jenny sat down to observe their reactions. When she looked at Antoni she knew that something was wrong. The expression on his face clearly showed his disappointment with his mark. Antoni is a bright student and one of the most popular children in the classroom. While his immaturity and forgetfulness are often very irritating, Jenny admires his enthusiasm and social skills. She is also impressed with his artwork, in which he seems to take great pride. Not surprisingly, Antoni is considered to be the class artist by his fellow students.

Jenny quickly checked her mark book. Antoni's mark was certainly very good, one of the highest in the class: 16 out of 20 for the story and 17 out of 20 for illustrations. Jenny was sure that she had praised Antoni in her comments. What could be the problem? As Jenny approached Antoni's desk, the bell rang. Antoni threw his book on the floor and ran out of the classroom. She picked up the book and read the comments that she had written last night: "Great job,

Antoni! I really liked your story and your illustrations are wonderful. Keep up the good work!" Jenny was puzzled. What could have upset Antoni? She looked around and noticed that Antoni was not the only one who seemed to have not responded well to her evaluation. She overheard Kaari saying to Madison as she pointed to the note that Jenny attached to her book, "Look at that. This doesn't make any sense!"

GENERAL REFERENCES

Eby, J., & Kujawa, E. (1994). Assessing student accomplishment. In *Reflective planning, teaching, and evaluation: K–12* (pp. 249–274). Toronto: Maxwell Macmillan.

Greidberg, H., & Driscoll, A. (1996). Assessment of learning: Let me count the ways. In *Universal teaching strategies* (2nd. ed.) (pp. 377–406). Toronto: Allyn & Bacon.

Popham, W. (1994). *Classroom assessment: What teachers need to know.* Boston: Allyn and Bacon.

SPECIFIC REFERENCES

Anderson, R. (1997). Suggestions for responding to the dilemma of grading students' writing. *English Journal, 86*(1), 21–27.

Gustafson, C. (1994). A lesson from Stacey. *Educational Leadership, (52)*2, 22–23.

Hansen, J. (1996). Evaluation: The center of writing instruction. *Reading Teacher, 50*(3), 188–95.

THE GUIDING PRINCIPLE:
Balancing Fairness and Opportunities for Success

"Students learn in different ways and at different rates." This principle sums up my goal of providing all students with opportunities to be successful. Perhaps I am naive and idealistic in my expectations. After all, this is my first year of teaching.

I was hired for a temporary, part-time math position straight out of university. I accepted the job in the hope that it would open the door to more permanent, full-time work in this school district next year. I had heard from my department head that many of the students in this school had negative attitudes toward math, and I hoped that if these students experienced some success in my classes their attitudes would improve. As I created my course outlines in September, I kept in mind the need to be flexible in order to accommodate different rates of learning.

My policy regarding assignments and tests is based on an article I read on evalua-tion. The main idea is that students should have more than one opportunity to show that they have mastered a concept or skill. If a student in my class does not do well on an assignment, he or she will be given the opportunity to redo it. If a test score is low, another version of the test can be written.

Just as I had hoped, my students responded enthusiastically when I explained my approach to evaluation. I really enjoyed teaching for most of the first term. Being part-time meant that I wasn't under the pressure that my friends who were teaching full-time were experiencing. The extra time I had for preparation allowed my lessons to be well organized and interesting and my marking to be prompt and thorough. I also had time to supervise the fall dance, sponsor the debate club, and sit on one of the school's committees.

The first sign of trouble was in October, when Ryan in my Math 8 didn't hand in two assignments. He also failed the subsequent unit test. Since I had to create a make-up test for Ryan, I asked all my grade eights if anyone else wanted to rewrite for a higher mark. To my surprise, the students who had B's and A's were the ones who wanted to rewrite. I administered the test to seven students over a lunch hour. Five students, including Ryan, earned a similar mark as they did on the first version of the test. One student scored substantially higher; one scored much lower than on the first test. When I returned the tests, Lily, the one whose mark dropped, started crying. "Please just throw this test out," she begged. I assured her that it would not affect her mark.

The next day before school, three boys from one of my Math 9 classes came to see me. These were three of my favourite students, and I greeted them with a smile. Ben, Lily's brother, spoke first: "We'd like to rewrite some tests."

I was puzzled. "Why? You are all doing very well." They explained that the top students in Math 9 would be selected for an honours Math 10 class. Apparently, competition was stiff and even a couple of percentage points could make a difference. "Besides," Ben continued, "it's worth doing the tests again. There's nothing to lose."

Right, I thought, nothing except my entire weekend spent developing new tests. "I don't think so guys," I responded. "There has to be a reason to rewrite a test." All three boys were visibly disappointed. They left my room muttering about unfair treatment and my useless evaluation policy. While I sympathized with these boys, I realized that this make-up-test idea could get out of hand.

Just how far out of hand it could get I found out during the last week of term one at the end of November. Suddenly, Ryan and all the other students who had missed assignments were handing them in. These students also wanted to rewrite tests on which they had done poorly. Here I was try-ing to mark the last unit tests of the term and to learn the computerized marks program for report cards, and now I had all of these late assignments and requests for make-up tests to contend with. To make matters worse, I noticed that at the top of one of the late assignments was Ryan's name scrawled over the erased remains of Jake's name. If Ryan was handing in Jake's work, how could I be sure that other students weren't simply copying their friends' assignments that I'd marked and returned earlier in the term?

I want my students to be successful, but I also want them to take responsibility for their own learning. I'm wondering if my evaluation policy just encouraged students to be irresponsible.

GENERAL REFERENCES

Arends, R. (1994). Assessment and evaluation. In *Learning to teach* (pp. 211–236). New York: McGraw-Hill.

Henson, K. (1993). Test construction, administration, and scoring. In *Methods and strategies for teaching in secondary and middle schools* (2nd ed.) (pp. 274–341). New York: Longman.

Popham, W. (1994). *Classroom assessment: What teachers need to know.* Boston: Allyn and Bacon.

SPECIFIC REFERENCES

Kohn, A. (1994). Grading: The issue is not how but why. *Educational Leadership, 52*(2), 38–41.

Krumboltz, J., & Yeh, C. (1996). Competitive grading sabotages good teaching. *Phi Delta Kappan, 78*(4), 324–326.

Seeley, M. (1994). The mismatch between assessment and grading. *Educational Leadership, 52*(2), 4–6.

MISSING THE POINT:
Matching Instruction with Evaluation Strategies

19

Amy Lanier is a business education student-teacher at Mountain View Secondary School, a large urban high school. She has been on extended practicum for six weeks and has developed good working relationships with her students, sponsor teachers, and faculty adviser. From the start, Amy competently took over a Marketing 12 class of 26 students with diverse cultural and ethnic backgrounds. Amy was particularly well organized and knowledgeable of her subject area. Before beginning the teacher education program, she had worked for six years as an account manager in a large accounting firm. Since coming to Mountain View, she has found the experience of working with high-school students very rewarding, and her students were responding well to her instruction.

Amy walked toward her Marketing 12 classroom with a sense of eagerness and anticipation. Her main objective for the lesson was to have students explore the advertising practices of a large international company. Before her students arrived, she carefully wrote the outline for the lesson on the chalkboard.

OUTLINE

1. Return quiz
2. Introduction — Advertising Terms (mini-lecture)
   a) Examples (Planet Hollywood, McDonalds, etc.)
3. Film — Benetton
4. Follow-up Q&A
5. Case Study — Analysis (25 marks) Due one week from today

After welcoming her students and returning their quiz, Amy introduced some basic advertising concepts. The mini-lecture lasted for approximately fifteen minutes. During these mini-lectures, a format that Amy liked, she did an excellent job of engaging most of her students. It was obvious that her students found these lectures highly entertaining as well as a valuable source of information.

As part of her lessons, Amy often told stories about her business experiences, coupled with textbook readings and articles. Amy noticed that her students were developing disciplined work habits.

After fifteen minutes, Amy was satisfied that her students were ready to view the film clip of Benetton, a high-profile company familiar to all of her students. Just before the film, Amy distributed a handout that was intended to help students focus on key issues. Amy wanted them to pay particular attention to the type of language and arguments put forth by company executives, as well as the controversial and often provocative images that Benetton used in their advertising campaigns.

During the film, Amy stopped the tape three or four times to emphasize a key point to her students. On these occasions, she purposefully highlighted sections of the textbook that would be helpful to students when they did the case study analysis.

When the film ended, Amy expected her students to have some strong reactions to what they had seen. She wasn't disappointed. Clearly, some of the images were controversial, such as the dying AIDS patient and the blood-splattered T-shirt worn by the Bosnian civilian killed in crossfire. Over the next several minutes, Amy and her students engaged in a spirited discussion about Benetton's advertising strategies. However, Amy struggled at times to focus her students on the key issues. She wanted them to analyze Benetton's marketing practices, and that meant moving them beyond mere opinion.

Twenty minutes before the end of class, Amy briefed her students on the case study analysis project. It would be graded out of 25 marks and be due in one week. Amy cautioned them about providing simple, one-dimensional answers. Instead, she expected them to provide a detailed evaluation of Benetton and the people who managed it. Each student was to answer a series of questions that Amy provided. Specifically, she expected students to apply the concept of the retail marketing mix (product, price, place, and promotion), as well as consider customer service and retailer image. Some of this information was in the film, but students would also need to apply what they read in the textbook if they expected to get a top grade. With only five minutes to go in the period, Amy reminded her students that she expected them to provide a reasoned argument to the case study.

As the period ended, Amy thought that the lesson had been a success. As the bell rang, Amy told them how pleased she was with their participation in the lesson and that she was looking forward to reading their case studies.

One week later, Amy became increasingly frustrated as she marked one case study after another. Something had gone wrong. Almost every student had missed the point. Most of them merely gave their opinion about Benetton, but neglected to focus on the issues and topics that were contained in the textbook readings. Amy was confused. What had gone wrong? At the same time, the lesson seemed like a success. What was she going to tell her students when she returned the case studies?

GENERAL REFERENCES

Arends, R. (1994). Assessment and evaluation. In *Learning to teach* (pp. 211–236). New York: McGraw-Hill.

Cruikshank, D., Bainer, D., & Metcalf, K. (1995). Evaluating students' learning. In *The act of teaching* (pp. 259–296). New York: McGraw-Hill.

SPECIFIC REFERENCES

Herbert, J., & McNergney, R. (1988). Teachers' planning for and implementation of evaluation in elementary and secondary classrooms. *Journal of Research and Development in Education, 22*(1), 39–46.

Simmons, R. (1994). The horse before the cart: Assessing for understanding. *Educational Leadership, 51*(5), 22–23.

MEETING WITH PARENTS: Challenges of Parent–Teacher Conferencing

Martha Lee, an art student-teacher, wasn't exactly sure what to expect as she made her way to the school gym to observe parent–teacher interviews. She was partway through her extended practicum at Sir James Elliott Secondary School, a large urban school, and was pleased that Grace Klassen, her sponsor teacher, had invited her to observe the interview process.

The first interview was with Mr. Franklin Tullock, whose daughter Sumra was in Grace's Fine Art 12 class.

Grace: Hello, Sumra. Nice to see you again Mr. Tullock. I'm glad you could both come together. Let me introduce Martha Lee, our student-teacher. She will be observing the interview.

Mr. Tullock: I'll get right to the point. Last term, Sumra had an A in your course. How come her grade has dropped to a B? You know that Sumra has applied to art college for next September. If she doesn't get A's, she probably won't get in. What's happening here?

Grace: As Sumra has probably told you, Mr. Tullock, she hasn't completed all the work this term and that's why her grade has dropped. I'm hopeful that her grade will go up next term if she puts in the effort. I think Sumra has a lot of talent.

Sumra: Ms Klassen, I don't see why this is such a big deal. You just said that I have talent. I don't think I should be penalized just because I didn't hand in all the assignments. They were early in the term anyway.

Grace: You know that's not true Sumra, some of the incomplete work is from the last few weeks. You know that. It's not just those early assignments.

Mr. Tullock: Hold on a second. Sumra, why didn't you tell me about this?

Sumra: Dad, I was going to …

Mr. Tullock (cutting her off): I didn't know what to think when I saw the B on your report card. Ms Klassen, can you explain Sumra's grade for me?

Grace: Let's look at my mark book. Okay, as you can see, Sumra did have an A at the end of the first marking period. You'll also notice that all assignments were well done, and handed in on time. This past marking period, however, there was a change. Here, look, three things not handed in.

Mr. Tullock: Can she make those assignments up somehow?

Grace: No, I'm afraid not. That wouldn't be fair to the other students. I have a policy that every student knows about and I …

Mr. Tullock (cutting her off): I don't mean to be rude Ms Klassen, but surely you could change your policy.

Grace: Let me explain. Because this course requires students to be working on several projects at once, it's really important that they don't fall behind. This is a studio course and that means …

Mr. Tullock (cutting her off again): I don't see what that has to do with your grading policy.

Grace: I was going to say that because students are usually working on several things at once, I have flexible due dates. For example, when a project is almost due, I give all students several reminders. I post the due dates on the blackboard and I expect my students to keep track of the dates. In my class, assignments are always due on Monday. For example, this last assignment that Sumra didn't hand in was due the week of April 14 to 18. That means that the project was due on Monday, April 14, but students can choose to hand it in either Monday, Tuesday, Wednesday, Thursday, or Friday without penalty. I'm not explaining this very well, am I? Let me start again. Students can hand in the project up to four days late without penalty. After four days,

however, it's a zero and I won't accept it. I've always found this to be a fair system. In fact, students really like it because it gives them the flexibility to hand it in when it's most convenient for them.

Mr. Tullock: Is this true Sumra?

Sumra: Yes, I got behind in one project. You remember, that's when cousin Zoe came to visit from Los Angeles. Then I got sick the following weekend when I had planned to work on the assignment. I just never got around to finishing it.

Grace: One of the things I want to stress to you, Mr. Tullock, is that I'm flexible and that on occasion I will extend due dates if there are extenuating circumstances. It's a policy to encourage students to be responsible for their own work. The policy is not cast in stone.

Mr. Tullock: Does that mean you will reconsider Sumra's grade?

Grace: No, not in this case, but I will tell you that if Sumra works hard this term and at the level she is capable of, I see no reason why she shouldn't be able to move her grade back up to an A. What do you think Sumra?

Sumra: Ya, I guess so. I'm starting to work on my photographic montage of downtown Vancouver alleys. It's going to be great when it's finished. I have some really interesting locations and I'm hoping to shoot some more images this weekend.

Grace: If you have any problems Sumra, you'll be sure to talk to me, right? Is there anything else Mr. Tullock?

Mr. Tullock: No, thanks for your time. I'll talk to you later.

Grace took a deep breath. There was no time to rest because Mr. and Mrs. Tam and their daughter Anna seated themselves in the chairs that Mr. Tullock and Sumra had just vacated. Grace wasn't keen on the way this school scheduled parent–teacher interviews. She preferred to make scheduled appointments with parents instead of the first-come-first-served method used at this school.

Grace: Hello Mr. Tam. Hi, Anna. Nice to see you again Mrs. Tam. I'm glad that you could all come together. Let me introduce Martha Lee, our student-teacher. She will be observing the interview.

Mrs. Tam: First of all, let me thank you for the wonderful job you're doing with Anna. We've noticed real improvement this year, and we think it has a lot to do with all the extra time you've been spending with Anna.

(The interview continues for 15 minutes.)

The next day, after school, Grace Klassen and Martha Lee discussed the previous night's parent–teacher interviews.

Grace: Pretty interesting night, wasn't it?

Martha: I had no idea what was involved. I was surprised at how many parents showed up.

Grace: Yes, most of my students have pretty supportive parents. What did you think about Mr. Tullock, Sumra's father?

Martha: I thought you handled his concerns really well. When the interview started, I thought he was a little aggressive, but as you began to explain the policy, and some of the other things, I think he accepted what you said.

Grace: You have to have a thick skin as a teacher, and I learned a long time ago that you can't take everything personally. But it's easier said than done.

Martha: At the end of the interview, I liked how you showed Mr. Tullock the variety of ways you've been assessing the grade twelves. He seemed to be impressed with your records.

Grace: Let me tell you, one of the best pieces of advice I can give you is that you should make every effort to assess students in a variety of ways. Otherwise, you might find at the end that a student's grade seems

out of whack with your impressions of that person's performance. I found that out the hard way in my first year of teaching. I was so focused on the curriculum that I forgot about assessment and evaluation. To make a long story short, at the end of the first term, I didn't have enough recorded information to make an accurate decision on my students' grades. It was pretty stressful.

Martha: Well, like I said, you seemed to handle the interview very professionally. You explained to parents very clearly the goals, objects, and outcomes for the courses. One of the things I'm a little worried about is figuring out how to design an evaluation plan for the whole school year. I mean, I'm not even sure what I'll be teaching. How do I figure that out? And the other thing we haven't really talked about is how to modify evaluation procedures and methods for exceptional students.

GENERAL REFERENCES

Cruickshank, D., Bainer, D., & Metcalf, K. (1995). Evaluating students' learning. In *The act of teaching* (pp. 259–296). New York: McGraw-Hill.

Eby, J., & Kujawa, E. (1994). Recording and grading student accomplishments. In *Reflective planning, teaching, and evaluation: K–12* (pp. 275–302). Toronto: Maxwell Macmillan.

Henson, K. (1993). Evaluation. In *Methods and strategies for teaching in secondary and middle schools* (2nd ed.) (pp. 375–392). New York: Longman.

SPECIFIC REFERENCES

Le Countryman, L. (1996). When students lead parent–teacher conferences. *Educational Leadership, 53*(7), 64–68.

Smith, C. (1997). The art of diplomacy: Winning the support of difficult parents. *Schools in the Middle, 11*(4), 37–40.

CLASSROOM
MANAGEMENT

C h a p t e r

21

A DAY IN KINDERGARTEN: Dealing with the Unexpected

It was the third week in October. Carol, who had just finished her teacher education program with an intermediate-grades concentration, was finally confident that her teaching career was on its way. Even though she had been on the teacher-on-call list since the beginning of the school year, the first few weeks had been very disappointing. She waited by the phone each morning with great anticipation for a call that never came.

Finally, in early October, she received her first teaching assignment, and it couldn't have been more perfect! Carol, whose undergraduate major was in biology, was thrilled to replace Mrs. Hampton, who was ill with the flu and whose grade 6 class was working on a large science unit.

Mrs. Hampton's students were quiet and attentive, and Carol was very pleased with their progress. They all had such a great time together that at the end of the week Carol caught herself hoping that Mrs. Hampton would take another week off.

On Monday, Carol woke up at six and, just in case, reviewed her notes for the next lesson with "her" sixth graders. When the phone rang, she was both disappointed and pleased with the news. It was not a call to replace Mrs. Hampton again, but to replace a kindergarten teacher at another elementary school in the district: Oakley Elementary. While she would have preferred to be placed in an intermediate classroom, Carol thought that a day in kindergarten would be a lot of fun and certainly not too much work to prepare for.

Carol made sure to arrive at the school well ahead of the first bell. She checked in with the vice-principal and was handed a short note with suggestions for the day's activities that Ms Liu, the absent kindergarten teacher, had left. "Silent reading, circle sharing time, and morning songs; classification of colours and shapes activities" — Carol went quickly through the list for this morning. She knew right away that some revisions would be necessary. She couldn't quite imagine how a group of eighteen kindergartners could actually read silently for any length of time without going crazy, and singing was definitely out. Carol had never sung in public, and she did not feel like making her debut today. On the other hand, classification activities looked like they might be fun. Carol went straight to the classroom and was pleased to find a collection of worksheets and some manipulatives that she could use with her students.

As the children began to arrive, she directed them to wait outside until the bell rang. This should help start the day in an orderly manner, she thought. Although they seemed surprised, the children followed her instructions. She kept the doors closed while she went over her plan for this morning, but couldn't help notice the increasing noise and commotion outside. When the bell rang, the door swung open, and the eighteen kids poured through all at once. "Slow down, slow down!" she called in vain, as her students rushed to the bookcase in the back of the classroom. "What are you doing? Get in your seats!" she commanded, raising her voice.

"Should we take our books with us?" asked a tall, skinny girl in a purple dress.

"What books?" Carol replied. "I didn't ask you to take any books. Just sit down at your desks and we will get to work." For some reason, the children seemed stunned with her request, but slowly found their seats.

"Good morning everyone." Carol began feeling a bit tense under the pressure of the eighteen pairs of eyes fixed on her and faces that seemed more puzzled than pleased with seeing her in charge. "My name is Ms Chung, and I will be working with you today, as Ms Liu is away at a district meeting." While children in the first rows seemed very attentive, Carol noticed that two boys in the back were engaged in a dispute.

"What's going on?" she inquired, raising her voice to attract the youngsters' attention

and moving quickly toward the back of the classroom. All children in the class turned to see what was happening.

"Michael said the F-word, " complained one of the boys who had a freckled face and wore thick, round glasses.

"Did not," replied Michael.

"Did too," the other boy insisted.

"F-word is a really bad word," a heavyset girl with a pony tail commented.

"Stop accusing me. You always accuse me of things," responded Michael.

"You said it, you did!" The freckled-face boy was close to tears.

"Can someone tell me exactly what happened?" said Carol, trying to probe into the problem.

"Tim is accusing me. He is always accusing me. He always, always gets me in trouble. He is such a tattle-tale!" Michael declared.

"Tattle-tale is a bad word," the pony tail girl quickly added.

"You did say it, Michael," said a third boy who entered the exchange.

"Not true, not true, I did not really say it. I didn't say all the letters, I didn't."

"But you did say 'F-word,' " the freckled-face boy replied.

"That's not that bad," commented a boy sitting in the second row.

"Yes, it is," a few additional children offered their opinion. Now, the whole class seemed to be engaged in the dispute.

"Ms Chung, what does F-word really mean? I asked my brother but he wouldn't tell me," a boy wearing a baseball cap wanted to know.

That was about as much as Carol could take. "Enough of this nonsense. Let's get back to work," she commanded.

"Tim should apologize." The pony-tail girl was not about to give up.

"Look, I just told you, we're dropping this matter," said Carol, becoming really annoyed. She looked around and saw that the class was still debating the conflict and the noise level was rising.

"But Ms Liu says that you always need to apologize," the pony-tail girl insisted. In the meantime, Tim and Michael were punching each other, trying to prove their points.

"I don't care what Ms Liu says. Stop it, all of you. Stop it at once!" Carol was very surprised to hear her own voice. She never imagined it could be so loud. The effect was augmented by the dead silence that followed her outburst. Soon, though, the silence was interrupted by a quiet cry. Carol noticed a small girl sitting by the window with her faced buried in her hands.

"What happened?" she asked, making her way toward the crying child.

"Oh, it's just Claire," a boy with blond hair volunteered. "She's scared of noises."

"She's such a chicken," added Michael from the back of the room.

"Don't call Claire chicken. It's rude!" one of Claire's friends protested.

"Michael should apologize," the pony-tail girl piped in again.

"Shut up, fatso!" Michael yelled in response.

"Ms Chung, Ms Chung, Michael called me a fatso," the pony-tail girl complained in a teary voice while waving her hand to get Carol's attention.

Carol was leaning over Claire, trying to comfort her, only to see her shrink as if afraid of her touch. Just then, she heard a loud bang, and, as she quickly turned around to see what was going on, her eyes glanced over the classroom clock. It read 9:20. "This can't be. It must be later than that," Carol thought with an increasing sense of panic. "How am I going to last till the first recess with these brats?" She knew she needed time to regroup, to figure out a way to deal with this difficult group of children.

GENERAL REFERENCES

Cruickshank, D., Bainer, D., & Metcalf, K. (1995). How the effective teacher manages the classroom. In *The act of teaching* (pp. 367–403). New York: McGraw-Hill.

Kindsvatter, R., Welen, W., & Ishler, M. (1996). Democratic classroom discipline. In *Dynamics of effective teaching* (pp. 71–102). White Plains: Longman.

Lang, H., McBeath, A., & Hebert, J. (1995). Classroom management. In *Teaching: Strategies and methods for student-centered instruction* (pp. 101–122). Toronto: Harcourt Brace.

SPECIFIC REFERENCES

Boostrom, R. (1991). The nature and function of classroom rules. *Curriculum Inquiry, 21*(2), 193–216.

Evertson, C. (1995). Classroom rules and routines. In L. Anderson (Ed.), *International encyclopedia of teaching and teacher education* (pp. 215–219). Tarrytown: Pergamon.

Leinhardt, G., Weidman, C., & Hammond, K. (1987). Introduction and integration of classroom routines by expert teachers. *Curriculum Inquiry, 17*(2), 135–176.

C h a p t e r

ZERO TOLERANCE FOR VIOLENCE:
Rules and
Consequences

"Ryan, what happened, honey?" Mrs. Brock said as she leaned over her crying son. She had rushed into his classroom when he failed to meet her at the usual spot outside of the school. She had sensed that something was wrong — it was Tuesday, and Ryan had to make it on time to his baseball practice.

Ryan was now the only child left in the classroom. He seemed so small and helpless behind his desk; it was hard to believe that he was in fact one of the tallest boys in his grade 2 class. Mrs. Brock hugged her son, who continued to cry. "Mom, can we leave now? Please, can we leave?" he asked softly between sobs.

"Sure sweetheart, but why are you still here in the first place?"

"Mrs. Beasley wouldn't let me go," said Ryan, teary-eyed. "She said that I had a detention. I tried to tell her that I had a baseball practice and that my mom would be wait-

ing for me, but she said that I should have thought about that before I acted violently."

"Acted violently?" Mrs. Brock could hardly believe her ears. Ryan was an active child, but she had never seen him get into any fights or display a violent temper.

"What did you do, Ryan? Did you hit someone?" she asked with great concern in her voice.

"No, mom, I didn't. Please believe me." Ryan was crying so hard that Mrs. Brock had a hard time understanding what he was saying.

"I believe you, Ryan, of course I do," Mrs. Brock reassured her son. "Let's go home and talk about it later, honey." She decided to give Ryan some time to quiet down. She helped him put away his school supplies and gently led him out of the classroom.

While her voice sounded calm and relaxed, Mrs. Brock was ready to explode.

"Where was Ryan's teacher? Why had no one called her to report the incident? What really happened?" She wanted to get answers to these questions, but she felt that for the moment calming down her son was more important than satisfying her curiosity. They slowly walked across the school grounds toward her car. Ryan was still crying softly, leaning on his mother's arm.

"Mom, can I skip the practice today?" he asked. "I just want to go home."

"Sure Ryan, that's no problem," Mrs. Brock replied.

By the time they reached the driveway in front of their house, Ryan's eyes were finally dry. "I hate my school, mom," he declared. "Can I go to a different school tomorrow?"

"Come on, Ryan, let's first talk about what happened today. Perhaps we can find a way to make you like your school again. Remember, just this morning you were really excited about seeing all your friends." Mrs. Brock tried to shift Ryan's attention toward more positive aspects of his school experience. "Wouldn't you miss Boris and Theo and George?"

"Oh mom, you don't understand." Ryan was again on the verge of tears. "This has nothing to do with my friends. It's just Mrs. Beasley. She is so mean, so mean to me!"

"Do you want to tell me what happened today?" Mrs. Brock encouraged Ryan to tell the story.

"Well, we were playing soccer during recess and I was checking Lewis and I accidentally tripped him. He fell and started crying and began to blame me for tripping him on purpose. I told him it was an accident, and I even said I was sorry, but he kept blaming me. And then he got up and punched me hard in the stomach. He was really, really angry. So Boris pushed him back because he is my best friend. Lewis screamed and started to cry again and I

called him a crybaby. And this made him even more angry and he wanted to kick me, but I ran away. But Mrs. Kim caught me and she took us all into the office. And because the principal was away, she called our teacher, Mrs. Beasley. And when Mrs. Beasley came, she had us all tell the story. And then she started blaming everything on me and Boris. She said that we were violent and that the school had this new 'zero tolerance for violence' thing. I'm not sure what that means, but Mrs. Beasley said something about not tolerating me and Boris. I tried to explain that I didn't push or punch anybody, and that I really didn't trip Lewis on purpose. I think that she believed me, but she said that I shouldn't have called Lewis a crybaby because calling people names like that is violence. But, mom, I didn't know that 'crybaby' is a bad word. It's not a really bad word. But she still told me that I had to have a detention because it made Lewis really upset. She said that I was really mean to talk to Lewis like that. And she called Boris's mom, and he may be suspended because he punched Lewis. But I don't see why Lewis can get away with punching Boris. This is so unfair! And I wasn't allowed to leave the classroom for lunch, either. I had to sit at my desk all the time. I wanted to go to the bathroom, but I was scared to leave because I didn't want to get Mrs. Beasley upset at me even more." Ryan began to cry again. "And my stomach started to hurt, and I had to miss the choir practice, and now Mr. Wagner won't let me sing in the show." Ryan was in despair.

"Calm down, honey." Mrs. Brock hugged her son again. "Let me get it straight. You were not allowed to go to the choir practice?"

"That's right, mom. Mrs. Beasley said that a detention was a detention and if I had to miss choir that was just too bad."

"And then she gave you another detention after school?" Mrs. Brock was becoming even more annoyed with the whole story.

"Yes, she said that I did something really wrong, that the school had rules, and that I had to stay at my desk after school for half an hour. Mom, did I stay half an hour? I don't want her to get mad at me again. She can be so mean, mom! I don't want to go back to that school, mom. Please, please, I don't want to go back." Ryan was again very upset.

When Mrs. Brock finally managed to calm Ryan down, she wanted to call the school to discuss the incident with Mrs. Beasley. But by the time she got on the phone, Mrs. Beasley had already left the school. However, she was able to talk to the school secretary, who confirmed Ryan's story.

"We have a strict 'zero tolerance for violence' policy," the secretary explained, "and it covers verbal abuse. Do you wish to make an appointment with Mrs. Beasley for tomorrow?" she inquired.

GENERAL REFERENCES

Arends, R. (1994). Classroom management. In *Learning to teach* (pp. 173–209). New York: McGraw-Hill.

Kindsvatter, R., Welen, W., & Ishler, M. (1996). Democratic classroom discipline. In *Dynamics of effective teaching* (pp. 71–102). White Plains: Longman.

Lang, H., McBeath, A., & Hebert, J. (1995). Classroom management. In *Teaching: Strategies and methods for student-centered instruction* (pp. 101–122). Toronto: Harcourt Brace.

SPECIFIC REFERENCES

Glaser, W. (1986). *Control theory in the classroom.* New York: Harper & Row.

Ornstein, A. (1990). Classroom management and discipline. In *Strategies for effective teaching* (pp. 55–108). New York: HarperCollins.

Shakeshaft, C., Mandel, L., Johnson, Y., Sawyer, J., Hergemother, M., & Barber, E. (1997). Boys call me cow. *Educational Leadership, 55*(2), 22–25.

23

TEACHER-ON-CALL TROUBLES:
Managing without a Plan

"I'm never going back there," Georges announced.

"You're always grouchy when you're hungry," his girlfriend Nathalie retorted. "Have some nachos and tell me your teacher-on-call troubles." She gestured to the waiter to bring another drink. Most of the waiters at this Mexican café knew Georges and Nathalie because they often met here after work on Fridays.

"I was over at Fountain Middle School today," Georges began. "When I got the phone call this morning, I was told that I'd be teaching French 7 and 8 as well as one class of Girls Physical Education 8."

"No wonder you're hungry; you got some exercise today," Nathalie quipped. "What's the problem? I'd think that PE would be a chance to have fun with the kids rather than drilling them with French grammar."

"First of all, French isn't just about teaching grammar," Georges explained. "And, I'll have you know, the French classes I teach are a lot of fun. In fact, the four French classes I taught today went great. I had the grade sevens involved in role-playing, and they were fantastic."

"So if you were wonderful and your students were wonderful, why don't you want to teach at Fountain again?" Nathalie inquired.

"The grade eights there are crazy, especially the girls. They were manageable within the confines of a classroom, but when I tried to teach them in the gym, they were out of control. PE was the last block of the day. By the time I rushed from the French classroom to the PE office to change my shoes, the girls were already in the gym running around and playing with basketballs. I grabbed a whistle and the PE schedule from the desk and ran into the gym. The noise was unbelievable. Imagine the sound of 25 basketballs bouncing and 25 girls yelling. I blew the whistle because it seemed like a PE teacher thing to do. The whistle actually worked for a minute: the balls stopped bouncing and the girls looked at me. But within a couple of seconds they were back at it, as though I wasn't even there. I decided that I might as well just let them play around while I figured out what I was going to do. I hadn't been left much of a lesson plan by the regular teacher, just a page labelled 'PE schedule' that listed 'gym – basketball – foul shots' under today's date."

"You weren't given much to work with," Nathalie sympathized.

"No, but as a TOC I'm used to having to think on my feet. For French, I'm pretty good at it because I understand the goals of the program and I have lots of teaching strategies. I felt a little lost, though, having to teach basketball without a plan."

"You play basketball at the community centre," said Nathalie.

"Yes, but that didn't seem to help when it came to teaching foul shooting to 13-year-olds. And it certainly didn't help me take attendance when all the students were running around the gym. After shouting and blowing the whistle, I finally got all of them to sit down. Considering how many times I had to stop to tell them to be quiet, completing attendance was an accomplishment.

"I decided that the best way to begin the class would be to demonstrate foul shooting with a group of students. I don't know how much the others got out of the demo — there was so much giggling and talking. These girls find the strangest things funny. I told them to get into groups of five to practise shooting fouls. This activity worked for about five minutes. While some of these kids really needed to work on this skill, others were bored and demanded to play a game. I was getting really frustrated by now because I

was trying to work with one group that was having problems, yet these other groups kept complaining to me. Finally, I gave in, divided the class down the middle, and let them play basketball. Most of the class seemed keen to play, but some girls refused to leave the bench. No amount of cajoling from me could get them onto the floor."

Nathalie interrupted: "They sound like me at that age. I was so concerned about not looking stupid in front of my peers that I was afraid to try anything that I wasn't good at."

"You know," Georges continued, "I got the impression that there were three or four dominant students who were controlling that class. I certainly wasn't the one in control. In fact, about ten minutes before the bell went, the students just started drifting toward the change room. When I asked why they were leaving, they looked at me as though I was an idiot and said that it was time to get changed. I was left standing in the gym with 25 basketballs. I didn't feel like the teacher in that class. I think I've lost my credibility in the eyes of those students. I'm never going back there."

GENERAL REFERENCES

Cruickshank, D., Bainer, D., & Metcalf, K. (1995). How the effective teacher manages the classroom. In *The act of teaching* (pp. 367–403). New York: McGraw-Hill.

Lang, H., McBeath, A., & Hebert, J. (1995). Classroom management. In *Teaching: Strategies and methods for student-centered instruction* (pp. 101–122). Toronto: Harcourt Brace.

Parkay, F., Stanford, B., & Gougeon, T. (1996). Dynamics of classroom life. In *Becoming a teacher* (pp. 284–319). Scarborough: Allyn & Bacon Canada.

SPECIFIC REFERENCES

Comber, L., & Keeves, J. (1995). Demonstrating. In L. Anderson (Ed.),

International encyclopedia of teaching and teacher education (pp. 238–242). Tarrytown: Pergamon.

Emmer, E. (1995). Teacher managerial behaviors. In L. Anderson (Ed.), *International encyclopedia of teaching and teacher education* (pp. 219–223). Tarrytown: Pergamon.

Westerman, D. (1991). Expert and novice teacher decision making. *Journal of Teacher Education, 42*(4), 292–305.

Chapter 24

EVERYONE QUIET! — Gaining and Maintaining Attention

Ryota Oki is enrolled in a secondary science teacher education program and is approximately halfway through his extended practicum at Cougar Creek Secondary School. At an 80 percent teaching load, he will be responsible for Science 8, 9, and 10, and Biology 11. He feels really lucky to be paired with Viki Karovitch, his sponsor teacher, because she has been extremely supportive in sharing her ideas and resources. In today's Science 9 class, Ryota is planning to correct a test his students wrote the previous period. Viki, who is observing today's class, was a little surprised when Ryota told her that he was going to spend the entire period correcting the test.

Ryota: Good morning. I hope everyone had a good weekend. I spent the last two days marking your Chapter 6 test on chemical changes.

Lihn (student): How did we do?

Ryota: I'm pleased to tell you that most people did very well. You'll remember the

test was out of 50 marks. The class average was 34. In a moment, I'm going to return them in order of grade so that you will see how everyone did. The first thing I want you to do is to check the addition. Make sure I didn't make a mistake when I added up the subtotals from each section. If I did make a mistake, come and see me at the end of today's class. And if you want me to re-mark a question, come and see me at the end, as well, okay?

Carina (student): What are we going to study next?

Ryota: I'll get to that at the end of today's period. But first, let's correct this test. I want everyone to listen. It's important! Everyone, stop what you're doing and listen. Quiet! It's important that everyone make the corrections to their own tests because you will be retested on this material when you write your final examination. Everyone, quiet! Stop chattering and listen! We've talked about this type of behaviour before. You have to pay attention when I'm talking. Otherwise, we never seem to get anything done.

Yichuan (student): How long is it going to take to correct the test?

Ryota: It will take most of the period. We'll probably have some time left at the end so I can answer specific questions then.

It took Ryota less than two minutes to return the tests to his students.

Ryota: Let's look at the multiple choice section first. We'll go up and down the rows. When I call your name, give the correct answer, okay? Carina, what did you have for question number 1?

(15 minutes later) Let's move on to the second section. Some of you seem a little confused, so I want everyone to pay attention. Everyone, QUIET! Stop talking and pay attention. If you have a comment or question, raise your hand. Otherwise, listen to the answers.

Over the next twenty minutes, Ryota was interrupted several times by students. He was becoming more and more impatient, but Ryota maintained his professional composure and tried to manage the class the best way he could. When the bell rang to signal the end of the period, Ryota was approached by several students who wanted to know why they had lost marks on a question.

After school, Ryota met with his sponsor teacher, Viki, to debrief his lesson.

Viki: How do you think today's lesson went?

Ryota: I was pretty happy with the test scores but it was a bit of a battle maintaining their attention.

Viki: Maybe that's something we should talk about. I'm not entirely clear why you corrected the test in the way that you did. For example, why did you go up and down the rows asking students for answers? I'm not sure if that's the best way to do it.

Ryota: I was originally thinking of asking for volunteers but decided against it because whenever I've done that in the past, it always seems to be the same people who volunteer answers. I was hoping to involve more students, but it didn't work as well as I had hoped.

Viki: If you could do the lesson over again, what would you do differently?

Ryota: I'm not sure. They didn't listen to the answers. You were there — how many times was I interrupted? Somebody always asked for the answer to be repeated.

Viki: I thought some of the students were a little frustrated.

Ryota: I know I was frustrated. This class has been a challenge right from the beginning. Some of them just don't listen. I'm constantly interrupted or I have to talk over them. I hate doing that, but sometimes I don't have the patience to wait them out. I've tried everything. I circulate around the room, I make eye contact with students who aren't paying attention, and I've even sent a few pupils to the vice-principal. I don't like doing that either, but nothing seems to work.

Viki: One of the things I've noticed is that sometimes you get sidetracked by students. For example, when you were in the middle of today's lesson, Chester and Justin wanted additional marks for question 8. You had made it very clear to the students that they would have to wait until the end of class. And yet, you re-marked their question on the spot. The rest of the class got a little noisy while you talked to those two students. Then you reprimanded the whole class for talking, but, in fairness, what did you expect? They were waiting for you to tell them what to do next. It was almost as if you had stepped out of the teacher role for a few minutes. You can't forget about the rest of the class.

Ryota: I probably should have moved on. I could have talked to those students privately.

Viki: I guess the point I'm trying to make is that the longer it takes to make a transition — in this case, from one part of the review to the next — the greater the likelihood that students will misbehave.

Ryota: I've been developing strategies to maintain their attention. For example, I've been working on giving them clear instructions, I try to wait for everyone's attention before talking to them, and I'm using my voice more effectively.

Viki: Yes, I've noticed improvements on occasion, but I think today's lesson is a good example of how things can get a little out of hand.

Ryota: I'm not sure I understand what you're getting at.

Viki: I mean that there is a fine line in managing a class. I've always preferred the proactive approach. We've talked on other occasions about the problems you had with some of your classes because you didn't talk to them about expectations, routines, and rules.

Ryota: I think I've improved in that area over the last two or three weeks.

Viki: Yes, you have improved. I think, overall, you have done a better job of managing your classes since you've been focusing on some of these issues. But you seem to have more problems with this Science 9 class, although I've noticed similar problems with the other blocks.

Ryota: I think I've done a good job handling students who misbehave in my classes. Generally, I try to ignore the little things. Most of the time they stop talking when I make eye contact with them, but sometimes I have to repeat the strategy more often than I would like to.

Viki: At the beginning of the practicum you sometimes overreacted to students' behaviour. You appeared to be overly concerned about controlling everything they did. I think that approach was a little counterproductive. We've talked about this issue before, so I know that you're aware of it. You're much better now at maintaining control with a less direct approach. Let's get back to today's lesson. Is there anything you would do differently?

Ryota: *(hesitantly)* I don't think I would have spent so much time correcting the test. I think they were bored. I lost their attention after the first ten or fifteen minutes. Maybe I should have had them work in teams and given them ten or fifteen minutes to make the corrections. I don't know, maybe ask them to hand in the corrections next period and not spend any class time. I'm not sure. I can see the value of correcting the test in class time, but you're right, I need to think about how classroom management is often related to other things.

GENERAL REFERENCES

Arends, R. (1994). Classroom management. In *Learning to teach* (pp. 173–209). New York: McGraw-Hill.

Cruickshank, D., Bainer, D., & Metcalf, K. (1995). How the effective teacher manages the classroom. In *The act of teaching* (pp. 367–403). New York: McGraw-Hill.

Lang, H., McBeath, A., & Hebert, J. (1995). Classroom management. In *Teaching: Strategies and methods for student-centered instruction* (pp. 101–122). Toronto: Harcourt Brace.

SPECIFIC REFERENCES

Brophy, J. (1988). Educating teachers about managing classrooms and students. *Teaching and Teacher Education, 4*(1), 1–18.

Evertson, C., & Harris, A. (1992). What we know about managing classrooms. *Educational Leadership, 49*(7), 74–78.

Ralph, E. (1994). Beginning teachers as effective classroom managers: How are they? ... managing? *McGill Journal of Education, 29*(2), 181–196.

REBELLION:
A Teacher's and a Student's Perspective

RENATA CARMELO'S STORY

Friday, 3:30 p.m., in Gerry Dubrovsky's counselling office at Lakewood Secondary School.

Thank you for taking time to see me Gerry. I know you probably want to go home, but I really need your help with this one. You see, Jeffrey MacGillivray in my Social Studies 10 class defied me this afternoon.

This isn't the first time Jeffrey has caused me problems, but this time he really crossed the line. I asked him to do something, and he just said no. Maybe I should be talking to the vice-principal, but with this being my first year teaching and the fact that I'm being evaluated ... well you understand. I also know that the school policy on defiance is suspension, and I don't want Jeffrey suspended; I just want him to realize that he can't talk to me like that. So I decided to come down to the counselling office and see you.

This is what happened. We were studying the Riel Rebellion. I showed a short video, and the students filled in a viewing guide. I had planned to spend the rest of the class discussing the video. Unfortunately, the students weren't into it. All they cared about was getting the right answers filled in on their viewing guides. They weren't interested in discussing the complexity of the issues. I gave up on the discussion and collected the viewing guides. I panicked for a moment when I realized that there were still fifteen minutes left before the bell. Then I remembered that I had some primary documents that related to the Red River Resistance. If the students didn't want to talk, they could listen.

I was reading from the second document when I noticed that Jeffrey and his friends were looking at maps of a ski hill. In fact, Jeffrey had turned his back to me and was describing ski runs to three other guys. I couldn't believe how rude he was being. I wondered if he knew how it felt to stand in front of the class and read aloud. Thinking that it would be good for him to be in my place for a change, I asked Jeffrey if he would mind taking over for me. He didn't take me seriously, so I told him that I wasn't really asking — I was telling him to come up and read the rest of the document to the class. He looked me in the eye and said "no." I couldn't believe it. "Pardon?" I said. "No," he repeated. The whole class was frozen, watching what was happening between the two of us. Thankfully, the bell went. Jeffrey and the rest of the class left. I realize that I probably should have told Jeffrey to stay after class, but I didn't want to give him the opportunity to say no to me again. Besides, I was too upset to talk to him right then.

I don't know what to do. I can't just pretend it didn't happen. The whole class saw it. I guess I have the weekend to figure out how to deal with this.

JEFFREY MACGILLIVRAY'S STORY

Monday, 8 a.m., in Gerry Dubrovsky's counselling office at Lakewood Secondary School.

I bet I know why you want to see me, Mr. Dubrovsky. It's Ms Carmelo, right? I don't know what her problem is. She is always on my case. Like last Friday. I was finished my work; I'd even handed it in. There was fresh snow on the mountains, so Nelson, Chuck, Peter, and I were all looking at the maps, planning our weekend. We were talking, but we weren't loud and we weren't bugging anyone. Anyway, Ms Carmelo decided to pick on me. She just wants to make me look stupid. I thought she was joking at first when she asked me to stand up in front of the class and read. Mr. Dubrovsky, you know I'm a lousy reader. I had to go for extra help in elementary school because I couldn't read out loud. It's easier in my head when I can take my time. Anyway, the point is, Ms Carmelo was mad at us for talking

when she was talking and she took it out on me. I don't know why she hates me. I've never done anything to her.

GENERAL REFERENCES

Arends, R. (1994). Classroom management. In *Learning to teach* (pp. 173–209). New York: McGraw-Hill.

Ornstein, A. (1990). Classroom management and discipline. In *Strategies for effective teaching* (pp. 55–108). New York: HarperCollins.

Parkay, F., Stanford, B., & Gougeon, T. (1996). Dynamics of classroom life. In *Becoming a teacher* (pp. 284–319). Scarborough: Allyn & Bacon Canada.

SPECIFIC REFERENCES

Cangelosi, J. (1988). *Classroom management strategies: Gaining and maintaining students' cooperation.* New York: Longman.

Mendler, A. (1993). Discipline with dignity in the classroom: Seven principles. *The Education Digest, 58*(7), 4–15.

Zahorik, J. (1996). Elementary and secondary teachers' reports of how they make learning interesting. *The Elementary School Journal, 96*(5), 551–564.

About the Authors

Anna M. Kindler, Ed.D., is an Associate Professor in the Department of Curriculum Studies at the University of British Columbia, Vancouver, Canada.

Salvador J. Badali, M.Ed., is a Doctoral Candidate in the Centre for the Study of Curriculum and Instruction at the University of British Columbia, Vancouver, Canada.

Renée Willock, M.Ed., is a Teacher in the West Vancouver School District, British Columbia, Canada.